ALL WORK NO PLAY

ALL WORK NO PLAY

a SURPRISING GUIDE *to* FEELING MORE
MINDFUL, GRATEFUL *and* **CHEERFUL**

DALE SIDEBOTTOM

WILEY

First published in 2021 by John Wiley & Sons Australia, Ltd
42 McDougall St, Milton Qld 4064
Office also in Melbourne

Typeset in Roboto 10/15pt

© John Wiley & Sons Australia, Ltd 2021

The moral rights of the author have been asserted

ISBN: 978-0-730-39162-3

A catalogue record for this book is available from the National Library of Australia

Cover design by Wiley

Internal design images: © jamtoons/Getty Images;
© Dmitri Gribov/Getty Images; © Nataliashein/Getty Images;
© Petr Vaclavek/Shutterstock; © GardenProject / Shutterstock.

Disclaimer
The material in this publication is of the nature of general comment only, and does not represent professional advice. It is not intended to provide specific guidance for particular circumstances and it should not be relied on as the basis for any decision to take action or not take action on any matter which it covers. Readers should obtain professional advice where appropriate, before making any such decision. To the maximum extent permitted by law, the author and publisher disclaim all responsibility and liability to any person, arising directly or indirectly from any person taking or not taking action based on the information in this publication.

Printed in Singapore
M115368_150221

I'd like to dedicate this book to my mother and my father, who have been there for me with love and support my entire life. In fact, this could very well be the first piece of writing I have ever accomplished without my mum's editing skills!

I also want to dedicate this book to my partner in crime, Bree, and my beautiful baby boy, Sonny. You are my world.

CONTENTS

ABOUT
the AUTHOR

REMEMBER THE DURACELL BUNNY? The anthropomorphic pink rabbit that competed, and even drummed its way through TV commercials a while back? Well, the Duracell bunny was a mascot — or a series of mascots (were they a species?) that championed alkaline batteries coming out of the United States. Remember the line, 'We all know Duracell lasts longer than leading zinc batteries'? Yep? You've got this.

If you do remember the Duracell bunny it's definitely clear you aren't a digital streaming native. No — you've grown up a good, middle-class, free-to-air watcher. Dale is the closest human match to those pink, fluffy bunnies we saw on our TV screens. He's full of life and always on the move: always motivated to make the most out of his day. And his energy levels last eight times longer than anyone else's.

Dale Sidebottom is the creator and founder of Jugar Life (and Energetic Education), a multidisciplinary business platform that provides people with the tools to make *play* a focus of their everyday. Dale is a full-time 'play' consultant who taps into his 20+ years working in the education and fitness sectors to educate individuals, schools, sporting clubs and corporate organisations globally on the benefits 'adult play' can have on mental health and wellbeing. Not to mention the benefits 'play' can have on corporate productivity, on corporate culture and in the wider community.

HOW *to* USE *this* BOOK

IN THIS BOOK, DALE SIDEBOTTOM shares how play-based mindfulness, empathy, kindness and gratitude helped him overcome long-term struggles (and how this can help you too).

The lessons he learned about being mindful and the importance of play in our lives, along with evidence-backed science and play-based activities, form the backbone of the book. As an average Joe from country Victoria, you will be able to relate to his struggles, his successes and his journey to where he is today.

All Work No Play is divided into five parts, each focusing on an aspect of play: from the science of play to games that can bring you joy and connection every day. The first two parts define play and explore how play is instinctive and just as important for adults as it is for children. Dale cites scientific data and research by academics to support the power of play on our bodies and in particular our brains.

In part III, Dale identifies the benefits of play and shares play-based stories from his own life as well as research and anecdotes that back up his theories, while also sharing stories from the academics who contributed to the book — Professor Alison James, Richard Cheetham MBE and Dr Craig Daly.

It's a good idea to read the introduction first because this describes Dale's background and his mission, which is to educate and empower individuals to move and learn in a fun way, and is also the purpose of this book.

Part IV comprises the action-packed chapters, where Dale introduces you to his play-based mindfulness toolkit, which contains a host of his own games, activities, exercises, daily mission cards and The Daily PEGG ritual of play, exercise, gratitude and giving.

In part V, Dale implores us to never stop playing and talks about the mindfulness trap and ritualising play-based mindfulness.

The pages of this book are filled with fun and games for you to choose from. As some activities and games can be challenging to explain in writing, you'll find QR codes that you can scan (using your smartphone or tablet camera) to see them in action.

At the end of most chapters, you'll find a feature titled 'Last, but not least'. These not only recap the main takeaways of the chapter, but also pose questions for you to reflect on.

INTRODUCTION

IF YOU ARE 'all work' and 'no play' and find the pressures of life a bit much sometimes, then this book could serve as a powerful remedy. It may just be the springboard you need to start learning about, and embracing, 'play-based mindfulness'.

Whether you struggle with stress, find maintaining positive mental health a challenge or are simply looking to shrug off the cabin fever and COVID-19 fatigue of 2020, this book could be for you. Look at it as a pocket guide for fun: a reminder and toolkit that will help you find glimpses of happiness and fulfilment each and every day.

Did you know that there are three key elements in life that can instantly lift your mood? They are music, laughter and exercise. If you're on board I would love to share a quick little mood lifter with you to get the book off on the right foot.

Lift your mood

When your mood is lifted, you are usually a lot more content and motivated to accomplish goals such as ... reading this book. Not in a positive mood? Well you're not as inclined to benefit from what you're about to read. So, let's change that.

Before we get started I want you to put this book down and do *one* of the following:

> » *Play some music:* Chuck on your favourite song and for its whole duration, sing like a rockstar. It doesn't matter if you

have the best voice, or the worst voice (like me). Whatever the case, sing your heart out.

» *Laugh:* When was the last time you laughed out loud? If that's a hard question, it's something we need to fix right away. Whether it's laughing at or with someone (or yourself), laughter is proven to relax and revitalise stress levels — and your mood. Laughter can also be powerful in changing our perspective on situations. It can make people feel more comfortable (ease tension), reduce anger and bring more joy into our lives.

So, with all that said, here's a joke about my grandfather, Ken. Hopefully, this will fuel the laughter.

For as long as I can remember, my grandfather and grandmother have owned a farm in Yabba North in country Victoria. At the back of the farm, there is a huge dam ideal for swimming in. At one stage, my grandfather had put out really nice chairs and tables and planted trees around its edges to make it green and friendly.

One evening, he decided to go down to the dam to look it over. He grabbed a big bucket he hoped to fill with fruit on the way. As he neared the dam, he heard voices and excited laughter. As he drew closer, he found a bunch of women skinny dipping. He made them aware of his presence and immediately they swam to the other side. One woman shouted, 'We're not coming out until you leave!' Ken replied, 'Ladies, I didn't come here to watch you swim naked or make you get out of my dam. Carry on having fun.'

Ten seconds went by. He then held up his bucket and said, 'I'm just here to feed my pet crocs.'

» *Exercise:* It's no secret any short amount of physical exercise and outburst will get your blood flowing. Exercise is a sure-fire mood booster. It's a brilliant way to reduce stress and alleviate any anxiety flutters quickly. So, because this book is made up of *five* parts, I want you to stand up and do either five star jumps, five squats or five burpees.

Go!

The old me

I think it's important you learn a bit about me and my story before I try to convince you how you can change yours.

While yes, people often describe me as a battery-powered, un-turn-off-able bunny and see me as this joyous, energetic 'big kid', this hasn't always been the case. For a large portion of my late teens into adulthood, I was a person who was strictly 'all work'.

Come to think of it, I was an 'all work' kind of kid as well.

Growing up

Growing up, I was your average kid in Shepparton, country Victoria. A place just two hours north of Melbourne. Reflecting back, I was pretty darn fortunate. I grew up surrounded by a rather big, extended family and had two doting parents in Karyn and Kevin and two younger sisters, Kayla and Hannah. The five of us lived on Broken River surrounded by park land, bike tracks and a bunch of outdoor activities always screaming out for our attention. And I was just screaming out ... in general.

I was a kid who loved to make noise. I was a chatterbox and was always being told I could talk with a 'mouth full of marbles'. Something that (as you can imagine) got me into trouble at school in later years — and later in life.

I am forever grateful that I was able to share my upbringing with my two wonderful sisters. We had so much fun together, as well as many fights. They became excellent cricket bowlers and kickers of the footy because that's all I used to make them do!

But thinking back now, when I was a kid, I just had a lot of energy to burn. And a pretty intense competitive streak to match.

Country competition

In regional towns like ours, growing up in a hyper-sport-focused community isn't unusual. Weeknights and weekends are often dedicated to sport. And if you're not playing sport, you're socialising in and among your sporting clubs, often with the same circle of friends, time and time again.

Competition through sport was rife in Shepparton. And if you're reading this wondering about the 'Sidebottom' link as many do here in Australia ... We are cousins. That's right: all us male Sidebottom cousins grew up competing against one another in sport. Competing to be the fastest, the strongest — the best cricketer throughout summer and the best footballer throughout winter. Until one cousin made it to represent Victoria as Sheffield Shield cricketer number 836, and one went on to dominate for Collingwood FC wearing the number 22 jumper. I myself had the honour of playing two back-to-back years for the Victorian Country Under 21 cricket side and was the captain for one of those years, an accolade I hold with pride!

Looking back, perhaps because I was the first-born (and only) son in the family, I thought I had to prove my worth to my parents through sporting achievements. And as with many young kids — particularly boys — sport was a way I found I connected best with my dad, whom I adored. The man who also boasted an indestructible work ethic that went on to cement my own.

The kid-preneur

If I were a horse, you could say I was bred to work. Both Mum and Dad were incredibly focused and hard workers and instilled the same work ethic in me. Dad has always had one speed, and that's flat out. While — as you'll come to understand — this work ethic is something that resulted in significant burnout for me personally in later years, it was this mentality that saw me become a really thrifty young kid. Always chasing the dollars.

Before being able to legally work — between the ages of eight and 14 (even encroaching 15) — I had found numerous ways to make a buck or two. From age eight, I began helping my dad cut bricks when he was a bricklayer, earning $1 for every 100 I cut: back breaking stuff! I did the old paper-round runs around Shepparton for multiple years between the ages of 11 and 14, and also started my own little lawn-mowing business, somehow convincing my parents to buy me a flash new edger (which I still have today) and cover the petrol. So, you can imagine my profit margins here were pretty solid.

On multiple occasions I worked with my dad. When he left bricklaying, he bought GV Carports. He and his team would build sheds, pergolas and carports. Mum ran the office and administration and employed me during school holidays for $20 a day. These days were long and tough and taught me a lot about showing up. My role would start with Dad handing me a shovel and calling me Dig. I would then have to dig all of the holes for the posts and after that find the storm water. This could take hours. Once I had achieved these tasks, the boys would call me Doug, as I would have to fill all the holes back in again. I can't say that I loved this, but it did teach me to never give up as I didn't want to show Dad or his workers that I wasn't up to the manual work.

My final venture — and you'll laugh at this one — was at age 15 when I entered the counterfeit market. At the time, my cousin Sam was a wiz at computers (which weren't as intuitive back then as they are today). He found an overseas website that sold fake Oakley sunglasses, which in our town were all the rage. Seeing the opportunity, we quickly went into business together, purchasing a number of sunnies for $5 a pair. We would then take them to our high school and sell them for $40 a pop: an even better margin than my lawn-mowing business! I found the thrill of discovering new ways to generate an income intoxicating. And it was these moments as a kid that paved a way for my business endeavours later on in life.

Early career

When I left school I was hungry to get out into the world and make a good living for myself. Honestly, I was never the most gifted student in terms of class and studying or exams. I also didn't leave school with a strong vision or career path in mind — I was simply itching to explore what was out there.

After finishing year 12, I got offers to study Physical Education in Ballarat (3 hours south of Shepparton) and Myotherapy in Melbourne. This was a tough decision for me, made easier when I secured an AFL traineeship (through my high school) for a year if I followed the path to becoming a PE teacher.

This traineeship meant that only six weeks after finishing year 12, I was back at my old high school, Wanganui Park College in Shepparton, as a staff member. Oh to have taken a photo and captured the faces of those previously excited to finally see the back of me!

My traineeship year was one of the best years of my life. Supporting the PE staff meant I went on every outdoor adventure camp and ski trip. I could also choose to attend any additional excursion I wanted.

This was an extremely formative year for me, where I went from admiring the PE staff at Wanganui, to suddenly working alongside, and learning from, them. The following year I started what became my four-year teaching degree at the University of Ballarat.

Bad habits

Okay, okay. So now you're probably at the point where you want me to … well … get to the point. So, here it is.

Despite growing up with a rock-solid and supportive family and in a great regional town, I grew into a young adult (and eventually a man) who, at times, was extremely narcissistic and arrogant.

I had a need to always impress people and seek their approval. Perhaps this stemmed from believing the only way I could connect with or seek approval from my dad was through so-called accomplishments. Nevertheless, I lived life trying to work harder than anyone else around me. I was extremely materialistic and found myself always focusing on 'the next best thing' to 'buy' me happiness.

One thing I had also learned in school was the power and fulfilment I got from being the class clown. When it became clear I wasn't going to excel as a grade A student, I always knew I could make others around me (and teachers in some instances) laugh. So, as an adult I continued to try to entertain people. But when I was no longer comfortable with making a fool of myself, I found comfort in making fools of others. I would put others down in public to pry a reaction, or laugh at others in our circle. I tried to be the loudest person at each party. And of course my drinking would naturally amplify these inconsiderate and damaging behaviours.

While teaching, I was also building mobile apps and experimenting with different business endeavours. I was entrepreneurial, which, in some ways, saw me benefit from being someone with a sturdy ambition and eagerness to succeed, and a rather militant work ethic. But what I didn't benefit from was a healthy work–life balance at the time.

I would work upwards of 16 to 18 hours a day. Then I'd absolutely crash. And on weekends I would ride myself off with alcohol because that was the one way for my brain to switch off from my impending tasks over the coming week. I was constantly sipping a poisonous cocktail.

I did not own up to or take accountability for the way I behaved. I was incredibly selfish and only cared about myself and how my actions affected me or made me feel. And when people called me out on it, I was dismissive and blameful. This hurt my family, and it damaged relationships with girlfriends and close friends.

Eventually, this caught up to me in a very dramatic and life-changing way.

Burnout

In my twenties I got comfortable with making countless excuses for acting and behaving poorly. During this period of my life, lots of relationships I had once held dear broke down. And by the age of 30 I was divorced and homeless. I had hit rock bottom and began living in a dark void I found incredibly hard to get out of.

I do sit here grateful for the countless people who didn't turn their backs on me (even though it would have made sense for them to do so). Particularly my mum, my therapist Pat, and my cousin Steele and his beautiful partner Alisha, who gave me a place to stay (it was meant to be for 'a couple of weeks' but ended up being 11 months) when I couldn't admit to anyone my marriage had broken down.

I do, though, recognise that it wasn't just my selfish and narcissistic behavioural traits that led me into this situation. One other fatal reason I believe I found myself here was because of my damaging 'all work' ethos.

I was never happy because I was never present. I could not switch off. I could never relax, or would never allow myself to. I was always on the chase, and never feeling satisfied. I lived my life thinking that it was non-negotiable for me to work 16-to-18-hour days. I truly believed success or happiness would only arrive if I had achieved specific goals, or was able to afford luxury items. The only issue was that when I reached each milestone or goal I was working so hard to achieve, I wouldn't celebrate it. I wouldn't talk about it or feel proud of myself for it. This is because I had already set myself a new goal to fixate on and work towards.

My mind was always a million miles away from reality. And by the time I was 30, this 'lifestyle' hadn't solidified a fantastic future or provided a happy, safe environment. It had got me to a point where I had nothing. My life was all work and no play, and that literally cost me everything.

Looking back, I have genuine remorse for the way I acted. I hurt a lot of people and also deprived myself of finding happiness a lot earlier in life.

For several years, when I resorted to blaming others, I would project blame onto my dad. I never understood why I always wanted to or needed to seek his approval. And I couldn't understand why he (like me) used to resort to alcohol to block pain or the outside world at times. Truthfully, my dad was facing his own demons. As a boy, at 12 years of age, his own father (one of my grandfathers) took his life. Naturally, he and his entire family still tackle this daily and I never believed Dad had dealt with it correctly. So, I used to lash out at him when I was scrutinised for my lifestyle or poor behaviour.

While I won't go into this any further, I encourage you to listen to #150 of my *Energetic Radio* podcast[1]. It features my dad, and it might provide some further intel into our relationship — and perhaps make you see things differently if you're struggling with relationships of your own.

When I eventually got over being blameful and entered a stage of remorse, I knew saying 'sorry' would be meaningless without really changing or taking action.

---

[1] **Follow this QR code to listen.**

Introduction **xxiii**

And take action I did … but it took me a lot longer than it should have. Eventually I sought help and began to *really* work on identifying and unlearning damaging 'workaholic' and social behaviours.

Recovery

I spent about six months in a really bad place where I felt like I was slowly walking the Murray River without any visibility of the other side. However, the more I worked on myself, dug deeper, built a real understanding of my issues and stopped projecting blame onto others, the clearer the other side became.

Recovery was an extremely testing and trying experience. And also a time of revelation. I underwent counselling, which was hard but also extremely rewarding. And when I got to a place where I could admit I was suffering and needed help, my counsellor, Pat, spent every Sunday with me for 10 weeks, helping me to really dig deep into the areas of my life that I never wanted to go near. He also led me to an important milestone where I started to appreciate stillness and my own company. My mum is number one in my heart for setting up my first appointment with Pat — I wouldn't have had the courage to do it on my own.

The main reason I'm sharing these personal stories and moments of my life with you is because I want you to know there's no shame in seeking help — something I learned the hard way. It's still somewhat taboo. For that reason, I make it a mission to share the story about my time in counselling with men/males in particular so they know that there are many fantastic people in the world who will listen, pass no judgement and help you grow into the person you not only want to be, but deserve to be — for yourself, and others.

Throughout this time, not only was I able to deal with a lot of unresolved personal issues, but I was also able to begin identifying the things in my life that were absent, or that I wasn't prioritising.

One (and I'll boldly say, the most important revelation I had) was that somewhere along the way from my late teens into early adulthood I had stopped having fun. I had been living my life with too much seriousness. All I did was work, sleep (repeat). Fun, joy and play had utterly left my life. And this is something I acknowledged had to change.

I had to reconnect with my inner child. And that's when I began to experiment with ways to find real happiness and fulfilment every day ... and reconnected with play.

I began by scheduling 'play dates' in my calendar. Not only were these 'play dates' scheduled at times when I was alone, but I would also incorporate them into my working environments. For example, I began to schedule these 'play dates' when I was teaching students. Or, if I was working as a personal trainer or running bootcamps, these 'play dates' became part of the sessions I undertook with clients.

I saw an almost instantaneous positive change in my mood, my outlook on life and, most importantly, my experience with happiness on a daily basis. The more I played and connected with others, the happier not just I, but all of us became.

Systematically adding 'play' into my days became my form of 'mindfulness'. Play allowed my mind to stop and be fully absorbed in the moment. Play became the licence I needed to be fully present — to laugh and smile. And it was these short breaks that changed my life and kick-started my new journey to happiness.

Alongside these daily 'play dates', I also began to experiment with systematically practising gratitude. So, instead of waking up every morning to look at my phone and read emails, I would take 10 minutes for myself and answer three simple questions:

1. What am I looking forward to today?

2. What might challenge me today?

3. How can I make somebody's day a bit better with an act of kindness or giving?

I found that these three questions helped to shape my mood and outlook. They also helped me start to see the beauty in making others smile through simple acts of kindness. For too long, I had only thought about myself and my own happiness. I had never truly experienced the benefits of thinking of others first. This routine helped me to take control of my mornings before notifications and head noise began to consume my thoughts.

It was these short snippets of gratitude and play that quickly helped me form extremely healthy habits and empowered me to feel fully present, in control and content — all critical elements that eventually got me to the other side of the Murray. (If you would like to try these morning questions for free in an app on your smart device, I have created one for you. Simply search 'Jugar Life' on either Apple's App Store or Google Play's app stores.)

The new me

It's incredible what can happen when you are open-minded and in a positive headspace. I have lived and reaped the benefits, and now I make play and gratitude the centre of everything I do.

I'm no longer a teacher at an educational level — now I use what I have learned and my life skills to teach others how to be happy. In everything I do in business — whether it's running seminars, speaking on stage doing keynotes or holding corporate development sessions — I focus on shifting the way we perceive mindfulness. Mindfulness isn't just about sitting still, focusing inward and practising calm and quiet. No — mindfulness is about being present. So I coach corporates, sporting teams, teachers and individuals on how they can make mindfulness more fun, engaging and suitable for those who have energy to burn, and perhaps brains that are over-active and going a million miles an hour (like mine).

Over the years, I've noticed that when you tell people to find their inner child, to 'play' or to practise gratitude, they will resist. It can sometimes sound silly and be scary to be vulnerable and put yourself out there.

But when you create an epic game that involves teamwork, laughter, gratitude and — in its most basic form — fun, people of all ages get involved and see the benefits.

I'm in a moment of time where I feel incredibly grateful that I've found a way to incorporate kindness, playfulness and gratitude into my life. Several years ago, if you told me I'd be travelling the world speaking on some of the biggest stages about these topics, I would have laughed in disbelief.

But like my own personal journey, my outlook and goals in life have changed. I have one goal every morning when I wake up ... and that's to have fun.

Over the past few years, I have had the pleasure of speaking to students, teachers, corporates, families and sporting teams in more than 20 countries around the globe about the powers of what I call 'play-based mindfulness' and gratitude. I have spoken on the TEDx stage and recorded hundreds of podcasts with all kinds of people on their own personal journeys. But I'm still your average Joe from regional Victoria in Australia. I'm just now someone who has found my mission and my 'why' in life.

People call me an entrepreneur, and while that may be accurate, I think of myself more as a 'funtrepreneur'. For me, every day is another opportunity to laugh, play, smile and connect with others. And this is achievable and accessible to everyone — you just need to remain open to it.

Hopefully, as you read this book, you will be inspired to share my vision and spread fun and positivity with the lucky people in your life.

part I

PLAYING
the GAME
of LIFE

Chapter 1
What is play?

PLAY IS NOT JUST a word to describe an action or activity children participate in when they are young. Play is life.

When you think about it, play is one of the most significant actions for helping human beings connect (with ourselves and others) and experience moments of happiness, however fleeting.

It's also somewhat hard to define. Which makes 'play' a little mysterious and somewhat complex. Before I share my definition with you, I'll share a research-based response I received from Professor Alison James, who is also a professional coach, HE specialist and accredited LEGO® Serious Play® facilitator.

This is what Alison said when I asked her, 'What is play?' (and it's far more measured and insightful than what I've come up with!).

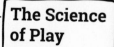

What is play?

This might seem like a silly question. After all, play is such a familiar word to us all that we surely know what it means. Yet theoreticians over centuries have tried to explain what play is, why we play and what happens in our bodies and our minds when we do. While their definitions may have common elements, they don't universally agree. So there is no single, agreed explanation of play. However, we can draw on the significant work they and others have done to help us understand the nature of play better.

Play is most obviously associated with childhood: aiding development, learning skills, practising behaviours and rehearsing what it will mean to be a grown up. We see play as having its place outside school or work; it's the thing we do to let off steam. We play to have fun and escape the shackles of chores, duties, work, study or other constraints. As a result, it is often seen as the opposite of serious activity, and therefore trivial or less important.

And yet, in 1997, renowned play theorist Brian Sutton-Smith distilled his 40-year professional fascination with play to reveal its complex and ambiguous nature. Identifying more than 100 concepts associated with play characteristics, he showed that play is determined by social, cultural and other perspectives. These might be influenced by upbringing, social background, education, profession, values and so on. Biologists, sociologists, anthropologists, philosophers, psychologists and others may all see it differently.

Neuroscientific studies, pioneered by Marian Diamond's investigation into the relationship between brain size and enrichment activities in rats, have also provided physiological evidence of the power of play. Her work and that of others reveals how play develops brain plasticity and function. Play helps us develop new neural paths and different ways of thinking and acting. Play keeps us adaptable and alive.

Animal behaviourists such as Robert Fagen, Patrick Bateson and Paul Martin see the key characteristics of play as being something that is freely undertaken and done for the joy of it. Play has no intended purpose, is often repetitive in nature and mimics certain behaviours (fighting, arguing) in a gentler form. We can see this recurring in human play as well. Sutton-Smith and others have made the case that play is part of evolution. This is seen in the way many living things have used play as a means of survival, trying out and adapting ways of behaving (interacting, hunting, mastering goals) in known and unknown situations. Play is not just learned, it is genetically programmed and instinctive. We do it not only because we want to but also because we can't help it.

Play is also about rehearsing important skills, dispositions and approaches to situations in safe environments such as the demarcations of a tennis court, a rugby pitch, a theatre stage, a hopscotch grid or an imaginary space. If you have ever seen a TED Talk, look at the red circle of carpet on the floor. That's where the speaker has to stand. It's part of the ritual. It's also a great metaphor for the 'magic circle', a special and protected play space separate from ordinary life.

There is debate about how play is defined and structured and how to categorise its different forms. Many forms of play are bounded by rules or have particular requirements or limits. These are often seen as games, but not all games fit definitions of play. In educational settings there is playtime, where children are free to choose their forms of play, and then there is play within formal learning. Adult or child, participants cannot always choose whether or not they will play, and there is often an agenda or purpose attached to it. The boundaries of what play is and how we use it are therefore sometimes blurry.

Play and playfulness can be seen as two sides of the same coin. Play might appear in a very obvious form (a game or performance, or a friendly sporting encounter) or it might

(continued)

emerge through our playful approaches to non-play things. We use these in every facet of our lives: getting babies to eat things they don't like by pretending the spoon is an aeroplane; through banter, in-the-know jokes, nicknames and teasing in our work and social groups; gamifying things for ourselves in non-game situations (if I finish this essay by 3 pm I can have a chocolate biscuit; if I manage it before 3 pm I can have two). Video game designer Ian Bogost describes this beautifully when he writes about his daughter playing around the cracks in the pavement (hands up if you've played it too) in his book *Play Anything*.

So far we have concentrated on play as purely positive. However, there is disagreement between theorists as to whether or not play can have a dark side. For some theorists, if there is harm or malicious intent, then the activity is no longer play. A kitten that pats you on the head with its claws in is playing; a kitten that swipes at you with its claws out, intending to draw blood, is not.

For others (such as, Sutton-Smith), play is not always a joyful affair. Think of office politics, business manoeuvrings, war games, initiation rites, the joke that has a sting in its tail. An alternative aspect of this darker side of play might be when it is used as a coping strategy.

We see this at work in highly dangerous or fraught situations where people use humour as a coping mechanism to deal with the challenges of their work: soldiers, firefighters, medics, for example. They don't underestimate for a moment the seriousness of what they are doing, but step back from it mentally through a play filter to alleviate the pressure. Dr Stuart Brown, founder of the National Institute for Play, produced significant data examining the relationship between healthy socialisation and development and play deprivation. Through this he showed that youths who had been deprived of play in their formative years were likely to commit antisocial behaviours or crimes.

Investigation into play over the past two decades has prompted and revealed an increasing interest in the value of play in adulthood. Particular methodologies such as LEGO Serious Play have featured in business and organisational development alongside the use of other play activities. Some of these include team-building activities through outdoor challenges or even the use of sheepdogs in leadership training. In higher education internationally, conferences, events and teaching techniques have all focused on the use of play. We are becoming braver in opening ourselves up to the possibility that play is far richer, more valuable and more complex than we first gave it credit for. We are also recognising that play is for life, not just for childhood.

So, as Professor Alison James suggests, defining play is complicated. But, to understand what play means to my life, and for the context of this book, it may help to understand how I view play, and what memories I have of 'play' as a child.

Like many kids, growing up, I was obsessed with LEGO. My two younger sisters Kayla and Hannah and I would spend hours on end building communities, businesses, houses and just about anything we could imagine. While we got pleasure and enjoyment from this, what we didn't realise at the time (obviously because we were kids and play was a natural instinct) was how this activity was helping us to learn to 'play fair', to socialise and to compromise. Admittedly, there was the odd occasion when Mum would be called into our playroom because I had made one of my sisters cry. But again, these more difficult, disagreeable and less-jovial times helped us all build the resilient natures we continue to benefit from to this day.

It's true that play helps us to deal with situations and to build the skills required to find solutions that work unanimously so everyone can move on without hurt or anger.

Another formative memory of mine relating to play is fort building. I have countless memories of my sisters and I building cubby houses inside our home. We'd create cubby holes out of pillows and almost any other material we could rummage up inside (or sometimes outside) our home. These activities taught us how to make solid foundations and the importance of having a strong base because without a solid base, our cubby, fort or castle would crumble under pressure. It aided our ability to be experimental and comfortable with the trial-and-error process, which is important later on in life.

As a child, I also loved to play card games such as 'Snap' and 'Cheat'. I got so much delight out of almost any card game I could master. In fact, I still carry around a set of cards everywhere I go as I find they always come in handy.

Thinking back to when I was young, I vividly remember exactly when and where I was when I learned the card game '500'. This particular card game still remains my favourite. It's an extremely challenging game and, as such, is extremely rewarding. Each hand you are dealt is different so you have to give the game a high level of attention. You also need to have a good memory and some solid tactics.

By the way, if you search 'What is Australia's national card game?', guess what comes up? You bet ya: '500'. So, you're bound to like it if you're from Oz.

'500'

Want to play '500'? Well, schedule yourself a play date with someone in your family, your workplace or your friendship circle.

Number of players

2–6: some say it's best played in pairs, as a group of 4 (2 in each team).

Rules of the game

It's easiest if I explain it to you! Just watch the video[2] when you're ready to play and I'll teach you! It'll take some getting used to, but trust me: while it will get full on, you'll be smiling, laughing and feeling energised from it for days!

The final example I'll share about my memories of play as a child relates to the primary school I went to. All three of us Sidebottom kids were sent to a Steiner School called Milbi, which is in Katandra West (on a dairy farm 50 minutes out of Shepparton). If you're not familiar with what a Steiner School or Steiner Education is, it's an approach to learning that inspires individuality and a more holistic approach than your more regular education. You're embraced and celebrated for your differences and your visible strengths.

If we put my young self under the microscope, examples of my 'strengths' were being 'loud', 'confident' and 'organised'. I'm sure 'organised' was a polite way to say I was bossy and a bit of a control freak. But instead of viewing this negatively, the Steiner

----

[2] **Follow this QR code to see how to play '500'.**

system recognised that I loved being a leader and encouraged and empowered me to be one.

Milbi was a great primary school. During my entire time there, there were never more than 40 students, ranging from five to 12 years of age. It was small and attentive, and everyone there was encouraged to play together no matter your age.

It wasn't clear at the time, but the communication skills, connections and understanding I gained from being friends and playing with students a few years older than me at the start — and then younger than me as I was finishing — has played an enormous role in how I communicate effectively with various people in different social and community circles.

At Milbi, we were encouraged to run pretty wild. We spent countless hours climbing the vast poplar trees — challenging each other to see who could make it to the top. Naturally, this probably wouldn't happen today (very unsafe!) but we all came out of these activities reasonably unscathed. And we learned a lot about the importance of making the right choices in the moment so that we didn't end up falling to the ground.

The reason I share these examples of my experiences with play is to aid in delivering my own definition. When people ask me what play is, in my mind — and through my experience — it's quite simple. Play can be doing anything with anyone, so long as it makes you feel completely 'in the moment' and free, allows you to let off steam and kind of makes you feel like a big kid (or a child again).

It's those activities that feel separate from things that can cause pressure, stress or tension. Play should be joyful and fun and something that is demanding of your full presence and attention. Play is a beautiful thing that should act as a mood booster, and it's something that has significantly shaped (and changed) my life.

Last, but not least

1. Teachers, professors, children and adults all have different definitions of play. And that's okay. Play is whatever you want it to be. It's non-judgemental and a friend to all.

2. Play is like brushing your teeth and eating a balanced diet. It's just as important.

3. Think of different play activities that you loved and can remember from when you were growing up. Are they similar to those of my childhood or do you have different play-based memories?

4. When you have a spare 10 minutes, think back and try doing something playful that you enjoyed when you were young. Imagine the look on the face of your partner or housemate when they come home to see you in the middle of the lounge room hiding in the epic cubby fort you built using all the cushions and pillows in the house!

Chapter 2

How play forms part of our life

NOW THAT WE HAVE (somewhat) explored what play means, let's have a look at how to categorise play and find out whether it's innate or learned.

What counts as play?

Just as it's difficult to define play, categorising it and labelling what does and doesn't constitute play is too. Play is subjective — for example, something that constitutes play for me may be a chore to you.

Professor Alison James elaborates.

Categorising play

The Science of Play

Trying to categorise what is, or is not, play is as problematic as trying to define it. Psychologist, educator and renowned play scholar Brian Sutton-Smith wrote that although we all know what playing feels like, when we try to define it through theoretical statements 'we fall into silliness'.

He found that trying to create a comprehensive description of types of play was impossible, as they are limitless. He grouped a significant number of them into overarching categories: mind play (for example, daydreaming), solo play (as opposed to play in groups), playful behaviours (for example, playing the fool), informal social play (for example, banter and teasing), play as part of an audience (for example, singalongs at a rock concert, lighters aloft in tribute to a song, chants in a football stadium, wearing marks of allegiance such as shirts), celebrations and festivals, contests, and dangerous play (for example, scuba diving). Dangerous play might involve the kinds of things that American poet Diane Ackermann lists as deep play, such as scuba diving, parachuting, hang gliding and mountain climbing. Hazardous pursuits take us into an altered state of consciousness – to exhilaration and beyond – which may even have a spiritual feel to it.

Different disciplines or professions may favour certain kinds of play: think of strategic, physical or wargame-related forms of military exercise. In my current research into play in higher education, I found that the kinds of play people are using in teaching and learning include:

» simulations and scenarios

» creating, making and building

» card, board and digital games

» puzzles, quizzes and brainteasers

» competitions and team play

» collaborative play for a shared goal

- » solo and group play

- » dress-ups and theatrics

- » play as shaped by unusual environments

- » outdoor and nature-based venues (for example, a forest school)

- » magic, trickery and sleight of hand

- » fantasy and imaginative play

- » parody and pretend

- » escape games and rooms

- » adventures, quests, tours and hunts

- » joke-telling and humour.

These examples are taken from a study of play in the university curriculum. If you look at corporate training programs or extra-curricular activities, clubs, associations and networks you will find hundreds more. And these don't even include the times when we are in non-play situations but are adopting a playful attitude and mindset. (Search YouTube to see Tim Minchin's commencement address at a graduation ceremony of his old university to see this in action).

Sutton-Smith includes some forms of activity that might seem peculiar to include in a list of play forms (such as babysitting) but may perhaps belong because they are conducted with a playful mindset. The moment forms of play become forms of employment (for example, professional sports) he considers them to be work.

Similarly, professor of psychology at Boston College, Peter Gray, also separates out a spontaneous ball game from a competitive, organised, success-driven Little League game: the first is play, the second is not because the play mindset has been replaced by the serious need to beat the other team for victory and prestige.

Gray differentiates free play — in which the players decide the rules as they go along — from more structured forms of play.

(continued)

Free play may also have a firm accent on the word 'free' — that is, the person doing it is deciding what they want to do and that they will stop when they have had enough. There is no objective or agenda. For Gray, free play is fundamental to a healthy human existence in that while a lack of free play won't kill like a lack of food would, it kills our spirit and inhibits mental development.

We play when we tinker with something: trying to mend it, create it, make it do or be something. Some efforts will succeed, others will fail, still more will produce an outcome that we didn't plan but rather like, while what we intended was a write-off. Through playful tinkering we come up with new objects, new words, new concepts and beliefs. Through our human creativity, our way of being in the world is not static; we invent new expressions that may replace or expand their earlier meaning. Old terms and phrases become discarded and after time are no longer intelligible to us, while some words that meant one thing only 10 years ago mean something else entirely but lose their currency quickly (think 'sick', 'wicked', 'fit').

Digital play through social media is rife in the form of memes, gifs, cultural references, echoes of themes, repurposing of images, text-speech and emojis. Our enjoyment of and fluidity with words is something that musician Stephen Nachmanovitch understands. He writes of musical improvisation as play and emphasises the pleasure of playing right now, as opposed to pleasure at some future destination. Play is the destination; it is all about the process. Improvised play helps us sharpen our capacity to deal with a changing world, echoing what we have heard already about play and adaptability. We can shift from work to play, or to any state, in a fluid split of a second. Nachmanovitch reflects this by asking deep questions about when something ceases to be one thing and becomes another: 'Where does the play of imagination come from? When are sounds music? When are patterns and colours art? When are words literature? When is instruction teaching?'

So, in addition to the myriad forms of play and playfulness we encounter, we also have this kind of blurry, shape-shifting play, which can appear in any aspect of our day.

So, we can see that play is multi-faceted, and trying to categorise or label it is somewhat impossible! Try completing the following playful assessment to see what play looks like in action.

A 'playful' assessment

Before I continue, I'd like to set you a task that Professor Alison James uses to challenge others. The goal is to prove that if you look hard enough, you'll find imperceptible traces of play in your everyday – even when you may not have classified it as 'play' before.

I want this to serve as an informative piece to help you understand just how difficult it is to categorise play. This may also help to inform you of what you (subjectively) do or don't classify as play.

Instructions

Keep a diary and record all your activities over a period of 24 hours. Really observe and scrutinise them, write them down and reflect on them. Then, capture all the types of play that you tend to undertake daily. Even when you don't realise it! Here's an example.

# Moments of play	Type of play
Travelling	*When I drove in the car, listening to music, I sang along and tapped my fingers.*
Exercising	*When I walked down the path outside my home, I challenged myself to only walk on the cracks that divide each pavement block.*
Working	*When I was in a meeting, I kept challenging myself to only look up at the clock when the minute hand moved.*

Born to play

It's important to understand just how natural and intuitive play is for us as human beings. Because, without a doubt, every single one of us was born to play.

You only need to look at babies, children and animals for proof. Think about the latest nature documentary you watched that showcased young orangutans or lion cubs. Or when you've seen puppies or kittens grow from a young age into adults. The one consistent thing you'll find among these examples — as well as in us, as humans — is how we all have a natural knack and instinct to play.

Richard Cheetham MBE (Senior Fellow in Sports Coaching at the University of Winchester in Hampshire, UK) says play is an integral part of being a child, particularly during their development. But it's not only something that's important for children. Play is critical for adults too and they derive many benefits.

Here's what Richard said in response to my question, *Is play something that comes naturally and intuitively to us as human beings?*

Is play intuitive?

The Science of Play

Play is not something just to know about and to understand, but to experience vividly, remember and feel.

There's a real beauty in being able to immerse yourself in a youthful sense of play and let those experiences 'shape you' — to inform, guide, teach and influence you and your future endeavours. Former UK children's television presenter, Baroness Floella Benjamin, said in an interview that she believes 'childhood lasts a lifetime' and so should play.

Children will and do learn on their own as they explore the environment that surrounds them. Play is an integral part of being a child and essential in children's development. And it is important to hold onto the essence of play throughout life — through physical activity or the arts, for example.

Curiosity — the master of invention — is something that comes with play; one example is when we use what is around us to find adventure and enjoyment.

'What if I do this?', 'How does this move?' and 'How could we use that?' are questions of intrigue asked by skateboarders and BMX riders in urban landscapes. There's no coaching; they are self-taught and intrinsically driven. Simply play for play's sake. Learning through trial and error with a creative mind that is free from directions, instruction, conformity and the expectations of others. A mind that can run riot in a moment of play.

These concreted play areas of discovery do not have age boundaries. They are not an exclusive domain of the young, but instead transformational learning places for adults too, where they become joyful, curious, passionate explorers of tricks and skills. Professional skateboarder Tony Hawk completed a two-and-a-half mid-air rotation (I had to look it up too!) at the age of 43 and described it as 'the best day of my life'. This extended

(continued)

his playful experimentation, which embodies learning through play, with the sport he started playing when he was 14 to adulthood.

Local off-road cycle tracks and downhill mountain bike courses are often populated with the 'big kids' trying tricks, landing 360s and mid-air 'supermans'. Board shorts and knee pads replace shirts and ties. This excitement or 'exuberance', as referred to by Frank Forencich in his book _Exuberant Animal_, is the powerful impact of play that results from a connection with our environment, described in such a way that you can almost feel the experiences encountered when we 'surf in the ocean and swim in cold lakes' and 'dance around the campfire'. We are surrounded by inviting opportunities for play if we dare allow ourselves to take advantage of them.

Play continues to be that place to socialise, connecting children to other children (and adults to adults) through a shared experience and without hierarchy. There are no elite play experts we feel we have to aspire to become, nor play academies. There is only the act of play. The tools and spaces for play may change, but play will continue to be essential in early childhood development and continue throughout life, where adults still derive the benefits.

Stand back and watch a group of children play. See play in all its phases, from improvisation to imagination. The evidence is there. The answers to 'Why play?' and 'How do you play?' are in full view through their behaviours and interactions. I have seen children turn bubbles into spaceships, trees into kingdoms, benches into rowing boats they climb aboard, and frisbees into the steering wheels of cars they dream of driving. From the simplest of ideas, often without toys or tools, comes the innate impulse to play.

In my mind, there's no doubt that we're born to play.

Last, but not least

1. Play is everywhere. You can be playing
    and not even realise it. It happens to me
    all the time. Like when I'm watching live
    sport and singing chants or theme songs,
    or doing the Mexican wave. Play-based
    activities add to the dynamic atmosphere
    of live sport and concerts.

2. Think about times when you were having loads of fun
    because you were playing. Did you see this as play
    before reading the scientific evidence and research
    in this chapter? I never thought singing the Essendon
    Bombers' theme song or joining 90 000 other fans doing
    the Mexican wave at the Boxing Day test match was
    play – but it is.

3. You'll see as you continue reading this book how play
    shapes my life, the work I do and my relationships with
    others. How does play form part of your life?

Chapter 3
Adults' play

MANY PEOPLE (MYSELF INCLUDED) grow up, enter adulthood and forget how to play. Or they believe that 'play' is something we grow out of and no longer need.

But that isn't and shouldn't be the case. As Richard Cheetham MBE spoke to in the previous chapter, adults derive many benefits from play, just like children.

Growing older, I certainly forgot how to play. And I learned that a play-less life is a hard one.

Growing older doesn't mean your life needs to become excessively serious or dull. Growing older means you have enough life experience to know what gives your life meaning. Continuing to revel in what you enjoy and what brings happiness and laughter to your life is the key to remaining youthful and sprightly — something I think we'd all like.

I love the J M Barrie character, Peter Pan: the boy who refuses to grow up. Life for Peter is adventurous and full of wonder, all because he chooses to maintain his free-spirited, mischievous and curious ways. Peter is determined to make a conscious effort not to concede to getting old. And neither should you or I.

Age is no barrier

One of the most content and happy people I've had the pleasure of knowing and watching grow old was my great grandma. When she passed away, she was 101. But right up until then, she would always play games. And because of that, she maintained her mental health, astuteness and youth far longer than many.

She loved the board game 'Snakes and Ladders'. You know — the one where you roll the dice to move up the ladders and down the snakes. Without fail, every time we saw my great grandma, we would play this. Whether it was one round, or a few.

I think that's one of the most beautiful parts about play: it doesn't depend on, or care about, what age you are or what age difference there may be among players. I was 10 years old when my great grandma was 100. The 90-year age difference didn't stop our games of 'Snakes and Ladders' from being any less competitive, enjoyable or exciting. And most importantly, it was a beautiful way for us to connect with each other.

The power of play

On almost every occasion, when I am working with a new group of coaches, teachers or corporates, play is how I break the ice to ensure we connect in the best way possible. I call this 'connection before content'. It's essential to build a relationship and trust before you start delivering any form of content in any situation.

I find that play helps people feel safe and comfortable with one another, as well as with themselves and with me. People's walls tend to come down a lot quicker when we use play-based activities. Meaning they're then likely to be more comfortable and confident taking risks, showing vulnerability and absorbing key take-outs from our sessions.

If play weren't the key element of what I practise professionally, it would take me a lot longer to form solid relationships and connections with adults — young and old.

I feel the power of play is relevant to almost every environment I walk into.

If I don't know people I'm in a social setting with, I will try to bring a touch of unexpected fun and play into the situation. The reason for this is simple. As soon as those awkward barriers have been broken down (and it may take me doing something silly — or slightly embarrassing — for this to happen) the remaining people in the room, or in the situation, feel safer about being themselves without judgement.

A great example of this in action is when I was in Kenya. This was some years ago when I ran a two-day African conference for teachers from all over the continent along with a couple of international teachers. I was pretty nervous.

One thing I am always starkly aware of when I hold any international conference is how thick my Australian accent can sound — especially when I get excited and begin to talk extremely fast. I still remember on the first day (which was a Saturday) at the International School of Kenya, around 30 teachers attended and when we finished I was desperate for feedback before the next day rolled around. So, as the first session wrapped up, Mark, who was a British teacher working in Kenya, confirmed my suspicions when I asked how he thought the day had gone. Great, but ... 'two teachers from different African countries didn't speak fantastic English ... and neither do you'.

Ha! Although he had told me they had all had a blast, it got me thinking about how I could make sure I built connections with the whole room and avoided isolating anyone.

Later that evening, two of the Kenyan teachers organised a meet-up in the middle of Nairobi for drinks and dinner. This is where I noticed that the two ladies who didn't understand me well during our session were also having trouble joining in on the conversation around the table. I identified this as my chance to try something different within a new setting. So, I decided to test an array of different games with the group.

The first game I tried was 'Buzz', which is a popular one many will be familiar with. The essence of the game is to have everyone form a circle and take turns counting upwards from 1 aloud. If your number has a 7 in it or is a multiple of 7 (14, 21, 28, 35 and so on), you replace the number with 'buzz'. This game didn't land so well with the group because it required too much 'thinking' and not enough freedom, so I quickly changed it up.

The second game I tried didn't need any instructions. The game's 'rules' or 'instructions' become really clear once you begin playing. I call this game 'Bok Bok' (although I'm sure it goes by a completely different name elsewhere). I started off as the 'Chicken Master' by using both my hands to make a chicken-looking face. I used my thumbs and index fingers to make two circles before using my remaining fingers as feathers. I then had to say 'bok' and signal using either my left or right hand to indicate the direction I wanted the 'bok' to go. Then, the person on either my left or right side (depending on my instruction) had to do the same thing: one 'bok' with the same hand signal, unless they wanted to switch the direction of the 'boks', in which case they would have to say 'bok bok' while lifting both hands to the sky! (This probably sounds ridiculous and confusing if you have never played it before.)

While doing one action and saying one or two syllables might sound easy, it isn't. It gets tricky to say the right thing, at the right time and with the correct actions. Although it's sometimes challenging, it's incredibly entertaining. And at this point of the evening, it was a huge hit and I was elated to see that the two women who hadn't felt connected in our first session were joining in and having a ball.

Our 'Bok Bok' game was so successful and engaging that the following morning (day 2 of the conference) the two attendees whose English was limited took the lead by unexpectedly saying 'bok bok' and starting the game all over!

Now, no doubt their understanding of my Australian accent/English didn't improve during that weekend, but our connection improved noticeably. Every time I looked at them, smiling, they would put both hands on their eyes and say 'bok bok' as loudly as possible. Everyone would laugh and smile. And it was those play-based moments that allowed us to transcend language, without judgement, and form a really good bond.

To this day, I'm still in close contact with many of those teachers, whose greatest memory (of a 12-hour session) was that silly game.

Occasions like this prove to me the importance of adult play. It allows us licence to be ourselves. It helps demolish 'walls' in the most tense and serious of environments. And most importantly, it helps unite us more than any language can. No matter what country of the world you're from, you can bet your bottom dollar we'll have a better chance of connecting and forming a bond through a game or playful exercise than by relying on you understanding my Aussie slang!

Because I see the power of play so vividly through what I do, it often leads me to wonder why, as a society, we seem to think we need to 'grow up' or 'grow out of' play.

When I discussed this with Richard Cheetham MBE, he seemed to grapple with the same questions and pondered why we don't seek the enjoyment of play in adult life as much as we did throughout our childhood.

Here's what Richard aptly had to say.

We don't grow out of play (part I)

To 'grow up' and take on board the trappings and opportunities that accompany being an adult, should we succumb to the gradual abandonment of play as an integral, be it less frequent, part of daily life? I question whether the nourishment that play provided before is no longer needed and the freedom, imagination, joy and creativity are confined to memories of our younger days.

Adults are used to conforming to rules and regulations. In play, rules are not set in stone — they can change from play to play, and from player to player. With 'busy' seemingly being the latest status symbol and feeling overwhelmed the new 'normal', has there now become a clear separation where we regard play as connected only to childhood and responsibility associated with adulthood?

There's an increasing belief that a shift in formal education from a curriculum focused on accomplishment, attainment and 'hard work' is valued at the expense of play, which is pushed to the fringes and the bottom of adult agendas. It doesn't count towards our grades and it is not easily measurable. Academic competence in literacy and numeracy is given priority over the powerful influence of play and the significant contribution it makes to young children's lives and their development.

Managed playtimes and supervised playgrounds where adults and adult rules are the imposters should be replaced with a 'Keep out — children at play' sign on the playground's fence. There is enough time for all that 'order' later in life when

(continued)

children become adults. This time is precious for adults too as they remember their childhood — a memory that lifts the corners of their mouths and lights up their eyes as they enjoy recollecting those moments. Play should not be deemed a luxury available only to a few. Moreover, if children do not learn to play as children, they are not likely to discover its value as adults.

Yet play needs adults. Children need adults as co-creators, as protectors of time, sharing knowledge and experiences with children through play. The strength of connection that comes through unstructured play is so important.

Richard also shared a colourful story of adults bursting with play, which has stayed with me.

Richard's 'Spartacus' story

The stadium was packed: 35 000 supporters at the Gabba in Brisbane. The first match between Australia and the British Lions, 2001. As good natured as the crowd had been, a policeman still felt the need to confiscate a large beach ball that was bouncing along the heads of the throngs of Lions supporters behind me. And then he uttered the words that he may just come to regret:

'Who does this belong to?'

'Spartacus', came the reply.

'So, which one of you is Spartacus?'

'I am ... I am ... I am ... no, I am ... I am ...'

And all with perfect timing, just as in the film. He faced around 20 grown men standing in unison with their T-shirts adorned with the word 'Spartacus'! Adults at play. A priceless moment: a joyful, laughter-filled memorable moment. I wish I could have bottled it. It's not just about knowing about play and understanding it, but it is crucially about experiencing it. To recollect, to reconnect and to revisit those playful opportunities. Holding onto it as part of our DNA and knowing that the dormant play gene is not entirely forgotten or abandoned because 'we had to grow up'.

The Ashes rivalry in cricket also embrace the playful nature of supporters who arrive on Test Match days in fancy dress from Elvis to cheerleaders and superheroes to beach lifeguards. The cloak of 'responsible adult' has been taken off and the inner child clearly let out for the day (however, at the Lords ground in London — a bastion of tradition — there are clear rules that forbid such behaviour!). Those who grant permission and those who don't are the gatekeepers of what is socially acceptable and unacceptable adult play. Same sport, different venue, different values and maybe different childhoods.

Richard goes on to say ...

The Science of Play

We don't grow out of play (part II)

I have only seen the plus side — the nourishing, energising association with play when adults lose the inhibition that protects them from the vulnerability of showing their playful side and allows them to revisit the freedom, imagination and joy that was associated with their early childhood experience of it. The demarcation

(continued)

line appears when we move into adulthood and gradually abandon play as something to have grown out of, something to look back on and not look forward to.

As the ever-increasing number of people who are experiencing mental health and wellbeing issues may identify, the accelerator pedal of life pressures is firmly to the floor and the road ahead shows no sign of easing, so maybe slowing down for play could be the non-medically prescribed intervention for alleviating the pressure and restoring our health. Historian Johan Huizinga stated that play is 'life transforming' and even a momentary release from the order and structure that comes with adulthood can be the refuelling needed for us to enter back into the world revitalised.

Adults need an excuse. They need an opportunity and the right setting to play — from amateur dramatics to the LEGO enthusiasts who prove that age is not a barrier to building, creating and preserving a piece of childhood. Being surrounded by fellow advocates of play allows flourishing and ignores disapproving eyes.

When I travel to work with coaches from different countries encompassing a wide variety of sports, they embrace play like meeting a long-lost friend. They are always only too willing to move into the 'play space' and relieved that a formal delivery is replaced with something more impactful and engaging.

One of the activities designed to connect people through play and to build rapport is to design and construct something using paper clips, straws, balloons, paper cups and anything I can add to challenge their creative thinking and improvisation. How tall can you make a structure that is freestanding, as tall as possible and as creative as possible? Each carries the same mark: 'You now have 15 minutes.' Enough time for me to sit back and watch. Paper clip bicycle chains, rockets with coffee cup boosters and lookalike Eiffel towers. No two the same. Adults playing, concentrating but laughing, talking and joking and all sharing in the delight of that play moment.

So there you have it. Age is no barrier to enjoying play-based activities. For our own wellbeing, play should be part of our adult lives.

Last, but not least

1. We don't grow old and stop playing, but when we stop playing we grow old.

2. The older we get, the more daunting and scary it can be to add play to everyday life. People don't want to be judged or show signs of vulnerability, which can be a side effect of play. It only takes one brave soul to initiate some form of play – opening the door for others do the same – and life becomes joyful, and full of laughter, movement and connection.

3. Think back to a situation you were in where a form of play would have changed the mood. This could be a job interview, a meeting or an awkward dinner with people you didn't really know. After reading this chapter do you feel play could have improved the situation? Would you try something if you were given the chance again?

Chapter 4
Play and our mental health

SO FAR, I'VE TOLD you a lot about my personal story, and we have explored the intricacies of play. But what we haven't done yet is looked at why prioritising play — in my everyday — had such a profound impact on my mental health. And it could impact yours too.

I love to talk about play and the benefits it can have on our physical, emotional and mental wellbeing because I'm walking proof of those benefits. This topic and its discourse is one I'm most passionate and positive about because I truly believe if you find a way to unlock your inner child, your life may change — just like mine did.

The health benefits of play have been proven not only through evidence, but also through first-hand accounts. For me, participating in and prioritising play is what helped me find and experience joy again after years of caring solely about work and leaving nothing else in the tank to bring about real happiness in my life.

Don't misunderstand me — I'm not saying that as soon as I started to play I instantly shifted from being a totally serious business guy to the person I am today. That didn't happen. But what I can say is that by injecting play into my life, on a ritualistic basis, slowly, over time, I started to reap its rewards. And I can honestly say it's what helped save me.

It's like learning to ride a bike. You start with training wheels. It takes time, and eventually the training wheels come off and your balance and confidence improve. The more you practise, the more steady you become until you are blissfully riding on your own. It's exactly the same with play: it takes time and needs to be enjoyed daily.

Now, before I continue talking about play and its benefits on mental health, I want to preface this section of the book by introducing a good friend of mine, Dr Craig Daly. Craig is someone who is always quick to offer his wisdom and insights when it comes to play, gratitude and the positive impacts both these things have on mental wellbeing.

Let's start off with a story Craig wrote reflecting on when he rediscovered the joy of a simple leisurely activity: golf.

Note: I am the 'new acquaintance' in the story!

Lesson 186.3

It was supposed to a be a casual game of screen golf with a new acquaintance. What it turned into was one of life's great lessons.

My golfing partner was dressed more for the Melbourne summer he had just left than the below-freezing temperature served up to him in Seoul that Saturday evening. His light, hooded top, combined with sports shorts and running shoes didn't seem like a sensible fashion choice in the snow, but it didn't appear to worry him. He oozed enthusiasm. As we walked to the indoor golf venue I'd located earlier that day, he responded to the strange looks he received from the locals with a beaming smile and the occasional wave.

A Korean colleague had mentioned the screen golf centre not far from our apartments. For 20 000 Korean won (about $25 AUD) per round on a course of your choice from a global list of more than 200 locations, in-built sensors and cameras would track your shots and use complex algorithms to accurately plot the location of your golf ball. All taking place irrespective of the elements, and with food and alcoholic beverages on call, it seemed like the perfect place to take a sports-loving Victorian. As we negotiated the crowded pathway, we struck a friendly wager on the evening's result, where the loser would be required to pay for both the cost of the golf and the complete drinks tab for the evening.

A multi-year layoff from swinging a golf club had done me no favours. My warm-up attempts at hitting a straight ball were abysmal, and my performance during the opening few holes mirrored the warm-up. I was a long, long way from my previous days as a four handicapper. The frustration began to build, and any thoughts of an enjoyable evening faded quickly.

Conversely, my partner was playing every shot as though it would be his last. Regardless of the shot he was facing, be it metal, wood, iron, wedge or putter, he approached them all with a sense of unbridled joy. It appeared as though the outcome of the game, and our wager, was the least of his concerns. It seemed he was just grateful to be doing something social on a night when he was supposed to be holed up alone in a strange apartment watching Korean Netflix. For a small man, he hit the ball incredibly hard. Every shot powered into the screen with laser-like accuracy. His carefree approach soon saw him establish a sizable lead of some 11 strokes.

I was resigned to losing, and losing badly. The blow to my wallet would be manageable, as would the damage to my

(continued)

ego. I would pass it off to those who asked as an expected result. After all, he was 25 years younger, far healthier and more motivated – a high-performance athlete who trained celebrities and led fitness workshops for clients on a global stage. Of course he would win. I was a 57-year-old, semi-retired education consultant with questionable health and limited patience, whose sporting achievements of note didn't take place this century.

Then the lessons started. Perhaps it was muscle memory kicking in after a 20-year hiatus. Maybe it was the four beers I had consumed in the last hour. More likely it was the conversations we had. We talked about how schools needed to reconnect with their students, how physical education class was both the most loved and most hated school subject. We talked about the importance of things like joy, affection, play and gratitude in the lives of school children. We talked about how people tend to be judgemental instead of being curious. We hypothesised about developing school programs that emphasised connection before content. And around the 9th hole, things started to change. I began to find some rhythm in my swing. Whatever it was, it worked. The more I listened, the more I laughed. I started to embrace what we were doing.

By the time we stood on the 17th tee (metaphorically, of course, as it was the same spot we had been on for the past two hours), I had cut my partner's lead back to five shots. I would still lose, I surmised, but at least there would be some dignity in it. At the very least I would finish the game with a few laughs, some new ideas and a sense of satisfaction.

Normally in golf, someone with a five-stroke lead with only two holes to play would play somewhat conservatively, thus securing the result in their favour. My new-found friend, however, was anything but conservative. He approached the difficult tee shot that required pinpoint accuracy over the virtual hotel just as he had done with every earlier shot. Seemingly without care, he stepped up and drove his ball so far out of bounds that it cascaded off the roof of the virtual hotel into the adjacent car park. His response? To fall to his knees in a fit of uncontrollable laughter.

He then prepared for his penalty shot, adjusted his aim to the middle of the fairway and proceeded to put his second ball into exactly the same location. Again he had the same reaction, and we both fell to the ground when the computer plotted both balls side by side in the car park. He eventually holed out with an eight, enabling me to cut his lead to two with one hole to go.

Our final tee shots, both to the centre of the fairway, basically meant the match was over. I was some 30 metres behind, and even with some scrambling play he shouldn't lose from there. The graphic on my screen indicated 186.3 metres to the hole, with a three-wood as the club I should take to successfully find the green.

What happened next could not be scripted even by those with a penchant for Hollywood storylines. I would later remark that out of all the golf shots I had hit in my life, this shot was the best. A relaxed, smooth swing gave way to the purest strike a golfer could hope for. A connection that exploded into the screen some 10 metres in front of me with both purpose and promise. The ball flew on an arrow-like trajectory and landed at the front of the green. Instead of stopping, it slowly followed the contours of the putting surface until it disappeared into the dead centre of the cup. Holing out from 186.3 metres for an eagle two. From the moment it had left my club it had not looked like missing.

The cheering, high fiving, back slapping and impromptu dance moves from the Victorian resulted in the proprietor coming to check on our wellbeing. Seeing the virtual stars still exploding on the screen as a form of recognition, she smiled, clapped her hands, bowed in respect and closed the door.

It would be 10 minutes before my colleague could contain himself to take his shot. Every time he would address the ball, he would step away, repeat 186.3 and start clapping again. He then put his second shot out of bounds into the other side of the hotel complex before eventually putting out for a double bogey. I had somehow won the match by two strokes. The money in my wallet would be safe until some other time.

(continued)

But the learning didn't stop there. The walk home was punctuated with aminated exclamations of 186.3. Back at the apartments later that night my friend, no longer just an acquaintance, took the lead and described our game in detail to those who had missed it. He talked up my mental attributes, focusing on my resilience to overcome obstacles, to trust in a process, to believe in myself. He overplayed the skill in my final shot, and underplayed the significant luck involved. He took responsibility for his wayward drives, but took great enjoyment from my win. Others congratulated me on the match result. However, for me, although I humbly accepted their celebrations, it wasn't about the win at all. As I sat there reflecting on the evening, I had realised that my swing was not the only thing I had rediscovered.

I was reminded that although I will never play golf professionally, I could be grateful for experiencing something that many professional golfers are yet to experience. I had rediscovered the joy one can have through activity. I found a person with whom I shared similar passions, and who took the time to ask for, and listen to, my counsel. By organising a hastily planned social event I found a better and sustainable approach for facing times of uncertainty, self-doubt and apathy. And the most important lesson? I found that you can dress in a light, hooded top, combined with sports shorts and running shoes, in the depths of an Asian winter and purposely radiate warmth to those in need.

The reason I love this story is because it's a reminder that not all things we do, and classify as 'leisurely', constitute play. I'm sure, at some point or another, Craig lost the raw joy and fulfilment he once got from golf. Until it quickly became something he looked at less as a 'play-based activity' and more as an activity where the pressure was on. The pressure to make the money attached with the pursuit of golf worthwhile. The pressure we put on ourselves to succeed and trump our competitors.

But his story, 'Lesson 186.3', shows that you can rediscover the playful, spectacular nature of activities when you learn to let go of pressures you or others build up around you. When you learn to simply sink in and embrace an experience and the company you're in, and be grateful for the sport or activity you're fortunate enough to be participating in — you'll be more 'free flowing' and 'in the moment', and take a whole lot more from the experience than just (in Craig's golfing case) a win or a loss.

Now, while I attribute play to having the most substantial effects on my mental health and wellbeing, I don't believe play alone is the way to achieve enhanced glimpses of happiness daily. When I began to see the effects play was having on my life (being the type of person I am), I started to research what else there was that would improve the quality of my life. In my late twenties and early thirties, I was someone who didn't have many highlights in my day. So I was eager to understand how else I could improve my life (however strange or wonderful).

Introducing 'The Daily PEGG'

Through my research, I found that, along with play, if I could include 20 minutes of exercise each day, and start and finish each day focusing on the positives instead of the negatives, that would make a huge difference.

After weeks of this, and when I was confident I was in a better headspace, I focused on making one person's day better with some form of giving or kindness. This meant that each day I had to have some form of play, exercise, gratitude (morning and night) and giving (kindness).

Now it would be amiss of me to sit here saying it was easy for me to do this day in and day out. But after time, these four things — play, exercise, gratitude (morning and night) and giving (kindness) — became daily non-negotiables.

And I continued to do these four things for one simple reason: because I felt one million times better the days that I did do them compared with the days that I didn't. And I still do.

Eventually, these four activities (play, exercise, gratitude and giving) took on an expression — The Daily PEGG — and this has become a ritual taken up by thousands of adults and children who needed an achievable framework for being more mindful, cheerful and grateful.

And I believe these are the types of activities that will have a profound impact on individuals and society, particularly in the aftermath of the events of COVID-19 across the globe.

I spoke to Craig about this and he shared his wisdom around whether we will see mindfulness and gratefulness take precedence in the years to come (which I hope will be the case).

You can read his thoughts next.

The Science of Play

Will mindfulness and gratefulness become more important in society post COVID-19?

If we accept that mindfulness is having a full understanding of the events that we encounter, then I offer a hopeful 'yes' to the question.

One thing that COVID-19 has done is provide a forced reminder for society to be mindful of changing circumstances. In talking to colleagues around the world, I am certain that the events of the pandemic have highlighted three things.

Firstly, the importance ascribed to certain physical possessions is grossly unbalanced, when issues such as stable employment, secure housing, food on the table, physical and mental health, and relationships are threatened. COVID-19 has made us view things differently. Having the largest house, high-end appliances and the latest model sports car means little when the support systems that you have in place do not deliver.

Secondly, the things we truly value can be taken from us. The effect of such loss is traumatic, often even more so when this occurs through no fault of our own. Dealing with such loss effectively involves complex and time-consuming actions. We need to ensure we have the strategies to move through the stages of grief, from denial, isolation and anger through to eventual acceptance.

Thirdly, while a rise in virtual platforms such as Zoom has allowed for increased digital connections, physical connection is necessary to sustain and nurture our existence. The restrictions placed on physical connection with others in global communities were a necessary action to stem the transmission of COVID-19, but the effect of such restrictions

(continued)

will continue to be felt for years to come. Events such as birthdays and weddings were shelved, workmates lost opportunities to socialise with their peers, and school children on home or reduced schooling schedules missed the physical companionship of their classmates. Both mainstream and social media reported on such things as Australian citizens being denied exemptions to travel overseas to tend to sick and injured family members, and Australian citizens trapped beyond Australian shores due to government-imposed flight caps. Becoming cognisant of the plights of others has led to a larger collective becoming more openly grateful for opportunities with those they love.

That said, there are excellent examples of increased societal gratitude to draw on, which I touch on below. Enforced quarantine in a raft of countries has made people acutely aware of the freedoms of a normal existence.

Having completed two weeks quarantine in Sydney when returning from South Korea, I know this feeling too well. The feeling of the sun on your back as you breathe in clear air against the background of a blue sky canvas is somewhat magical. Such an experience served to remind me why many dub Australia the lucky country.

Many have expressed gratitude for the changed environmental conditions that have resulted from the COVID-19 pandemic. As industrial output slowed or halted, global pollution levels reduced significantly. Waterways, such as the Grand Canal in Venice, ran clear for the first time in decades, allowing residents to spot schools of fish that usually frequent without detection.

Globally, a far deeper appreciation of the role completed by frontline workers has been evident. In Australia, public gratitude to doctors, nurses, emergency service and defence force personnel has become a daily occurrence. Examples are plentiful where workers were supplied required items without question, provided with food and drink at reduced or no cost, and had monthly fees for phone and internet access waived.

Similarly, remote learning and home schooling increased the opportunities for gratitude. The average person's awareness of the complex role of successfully promoting learning grew exponentially as did the demands and stress on parents who had to juggle home schooling, remote learning, work and family life.

COVID-19 caused many schools globally to reflect critically on their practices, with the call for TLC before ABC now gaining significant traction on the global stage. The fact that many schools are prioritising social-emotional connection for students ahead of academic performance is heartening.

Disrupted employment schedules gave rise to a somewhat unexpected outcome. For some, working from home or having a reduced commuting schedule resulted in families spending more quality time together. Opportunities arose that allowed parents to build a stronger emotional bond with their children, assisting them to navigate the uncertainties that life during a pandemic requires.

So, in summary, I remain hopeful that the ongoing need for mindful practice and increased gratitude is recognised, and actioned, as we move forward.

Craig's thought-provoking and eye-opening answer reinforces why I believe The Daily PEGG should be part of everyone's life in our post-COVID-19 world. There's a whole part of this book (part IV) dedicated to how you can include PEGG in your daily routine and how it fits into my play-based mindfulness toolkit.

But first, in chapter 5, we'll look at how 'play-based mindfulness' came to be born.

Last, but not least

1. Always go hard. It doesn't matter if you're five or 10 shots up in life or on the golf course. Always back yourself and believe in what you can do. I would still to this day hit my big golf driver over an iron to go for glory instead of safety.

2. Great things come to us whether we land two balls in a row at a virtual club house or we fail at something on multiple occasions. This is how we grow, learn and progress as human beings.

3. Don't be a human doing, like so many of us tend to be. 'I'm doing this, doing meetings, doing busy, doing deals or doing, doing, doing, doing.' Instead, be a human being, and start being present, being caring, being empathetic, and being open to new people, ideas and opportunities. Start backing yourself with your driver on the 18th and in life.

4. The Daily PEGG is a 'play, exercise, gratitude and giving' ritual suited for people of all ages — and it seriously works. We'll get fully into how it works in part IV of the book.

Chapter 5

The birth of play-based mindfulness

IF YOU HAVE NEVER heard the term 'play-based mindfulness', it may be because (as far as I'm aware) it is something I have coined myself off the back of my own experiences with play, gratitude and mindfulness.

I look at play as my very own form of mindfulness. In saying that, I don't think many people see play as a form of mindfulness. And neither does Craig Daly.

When I asked Craig, 'Do you think society sees play as a mindful practice?' he responded as follows.

Is 'play' a mindful practice?

The Science of Play

While my heart would like to say yes, my head says it's not that simple. The imperfect understanding held by society about what mindful practice looks like doesn't assist in positioning play as an important inclusion. That said, a more accurate response to this question requires consideration of cultural and contextual elements. The quote below from the 2011 film *Moneyball* is an interesting position to start with.

We're all told at some point in time that we can no longer play the children's game, we just don't ... we don't know when that's gonna be. Some of us are told at eighteen, some of us are told at forty, but we're all told.

While this quote is about baseball, and professional baseball at that, one can easily extend this mindset to how society sees play. I guess for me that quote sums up several things. Firstly, that play has a timeline. It's not a finite one due to a range of issues but yes, as adults there comes a time when responsibilities, physical ability, age and location exclude us from being involved in play-based activities. We lose (or seem to lose) the time, fitness, physical ability and motivation to remain involved in play-based activity.

Secondly, it highlights that decisions are often made for us by others. As we age it is our families and employers who have a mortgage on time. Meeting their needs may de-emphasise the importance of play to us — we are after all involved in meeting the responsibilities of 'adulting'.

There are always those who will see play as a form of escapism, and therefore would position it on the opposite end of the spectrum to mindfulness. Similarly, there are those who would argue the structure of some play — with its complex rules, traditions and formalised settings — is dependent on goal-based determinations, thus not allowing for the development of mindful tendencies. That position may be countered by an investigation into the states of mind encountered during play-based activities.

Yet in certain cultures, play remains a crucial component of how society works. Changes to rules and the introduction of seniors/masters/legends (call them what you will) sporting programs have allowed people to continue their involvement in play-based activity. Participating in these activities provides opportunities to experience the significant physical and mental health benefits from ongoing involvement. However, society's acceptance of activity (and therefore informal play) differs markedly based on cultural norms. As an example, having spent four years in Seoul, it was an everyday occurrence to see groups of elderly Koreans involved in informal activity.

Craig went on to describe his observations of 'play' in Seoul.

Seoul searching

The first walk to the summit of the mountain was, as mountain walks go, something I'd never experienced before. I'd done my share of walking, but nothing quite like this. When you started at the bottom of the Hilton suites hill, it was approximately a 12-kilometre loop, about three hours in length for those with average stamina.

At the canal you'd pass the exercise equipment being used by a group of middle-aged women — not unlike the equipment you might see in a park or at the beachside in Australia, but with one notable exception. It was all perfectly maintained. Not a spot of dirt or rust was to be seen, despite the outdoor location.

(continued)

The 12 machines worked as they should. The only sound was that coming from the chatter of the excited users. At the stretching station I watched with awe as a short, elderly Korean lady managed to place her leg onto the highest peg available, then proceeded to bounce up and down as if she was trying to break herself in two.

About one kilometre further on, the track turned past the waterfall, where the sounds of recorded Buddhist chants combined with continuously falling water to form a melodic symphony of sorts. It was here that the actual ascent began on trails manicured by the numerous Seodaemun-gu employees who were assigned that task.

A kilometre further on was the false top of the ring road, home to a number of badminton courts that were in full use. On the court closest to my vantage point I saw a young girl, perhaps around 10 years of age, being schooled in the mechanics of a satisfactory badminton serve by what looked to be her grandfather. The smiles on both their faces spoke volumes.

I kept going up what was now a serious incline. The sounds of bird calls, mechanically manufactured and delivered through rock-shaped speakers, filled the air. Another kilometre on and the natural springs appeared on my right. A number of fishing lines stood unattended as their owners slept soundly on the wooden platform.

You could see the expressway and its usually stalled traffic in the distance, but I heard nothing from its frustrated occupants. A little further up and the book café came into view. Not a café of sorts ... more a book depository where locals would swap their books with others at no charge. Large wooden chairs were scattered around the café — all in use with young and old seemingly engrossed in their reading material.

I found myself admiring the creativity of the locals when, sometime later, I stumbled on a collection of hammocks arranged to overlook a valley where sculpted trees formed a perfect horizon. Of the 20 hammocks, only one wasn't busy. The one closest to me played host to an older lady who was sawing logs as she slept undisturbed.

From there, each turn seemed to bring on something else to marvel at. No loose stones or decaying steps to impede your climb. No overgrown foliage to spoil the view. Just before the summit I found the outdoor weights gym, complete with free weights, dumbbells, ropes and an assortment of machines. All again in pristine condition. A little over were the hanging rings, set at various heights to provide a variety of challenges. The younger male on the highest rings would not have been out of place at an Olympic gymnastics competition. The twists, turns, and subsequent dismount were as close to perfect as one could hope to see.

A little while later I made it to the summit. The view was good, but I was more amazed at what I had experienced on the journey. I thought about my hometown on the Gold Coast. Would these sorts of informal mindfulness opportunities be available? Would the local council go to the same lengths to meet community needs? And if they did, would these things be protected from the local eshays and their constant attempts to destroy anything of value? I surmised that the answer to all three questions would be no, and the peace and tranquillity that had been with me the past hour was replaced with a sense of sadness. Surely, we should be better than that.

This walk became a constant release during the four years I had in Seoul. I met countless people, young and old, on the trail, on the courts and/or using the gym gear. Almost always I was met with smiling faces. It reminded me that, despite background, location or language, when we combine creativity and kindness, we can solve all sorts of issues. You just need to be willing to see the mountain and start the climb.

So, if we as a society don't view 'play' as mindfulness, what exactly do we see it as?

When I asked Craig, 'In a nutshell, what is mindfulness?' he answered as follows.

What is mindfulness?

The Science of Play

I guess it depends on which lens you use to view mindfulness as a concept. Checking recent publications reveals that there are more than 100 differing versions of what mindfulness is. Commonalities indicate a focus placed on attention, awareness and being present in (or returning to) the moment.

The key with most accepted definitions is the need to be _judgement free_ to obtain a mindful state. I tend to think of mindfulness more as approaching life and all its interactions with 'eyes and heart wide open'. One of the best analogies I have heard is that mindfulness is like walking into a totally dark room where a dimmer switch is used to slowly increase the level of light.

I view a mindful person as one who displays an acute awareness of daily life through something I call 'whole body observation'. This is using the five senses to frame feelings, words and actions. The key here is to do so with a curious mind as opposed to a judgemental one. This version of mindfulness allows for the accomplishment of tasks through complete attention, so it leans more to a socio-cognitive approach.

I couldn't have said it better myself!

'And why is mindfulness becoming increasingly popular in today's society?' I asked Craig.

Why is mindfulness so popular?

The Science of Play

I think the reasons are threefold.

Firstly, the increasing demands of day-to-day activity placed on schools, workplaces and homes have driven people to seek viable solutions.

Secondly, it is becoming more common (and accepted) for people to undertake an analysis of their broader social and emotional status. The level of education regarding appropriate responses to physical and mental health stressors is increasing.

Thirdly, there is a growing acceptance and appreciation that activities previously considered as 'alternative' provide tangible health benefits, and therefore are worthy of consideration.

From an Australian perspective, the rising popularity of mindfulness could be attributed to such things as the 2.6-percentage-points rise in the number of people with a mental or behavioural condition (resulting from depression or anxiety) between 2014–15 and 2017–18 (according to an ABS National Health Survey).

Suicide rates increased by approximately 9 per cent from 2866 (in 2016) to 3128 (in 2017). While instances of suicide are not confined to those with mental health issues, it is estimated that approximately 94 per cent of people who attempted suicide had suffered a mental health disorder in the previous 12 months.

A recent annual State of Mind survey by the University of Newcastle indicated that nationally, good mental health and wellbeing appears to be at low levels. There was a significant difference between males and females reporting stress, anxiety and depression, with females significantly higher in all three domains. Males were more likely to practise mindfulness as a preventative measure than females.

(continued)

Overall, respondents agreed that undertaking mindfulness practice helped in the management of stress, anxiety, improved resilience, creativity, focus and attention, sleep and work interactions. Increases in overall feelings of calmness and relaxation were also noted.

An explanation for the rise of mindfulness apps published by the American Psychological Association in 2018 suggested that Generation Z is likely to suffer from worsening mental health issues, and therefore will resort to alternative health interventions. But even prior to this, research noted substantial increases in yoga and meditation participation among US adults from 2012 to 2017.

The popularity of mindfulness apps rose considerably during the COVID-19 pandemic, with a combined increase among the world's 10 most popular English language mental wellness app downloads between January and April 2020 of two million – and almost 10 million downloads in April alone.

While this evidence paints a concerning picture of the mental health of Australians (and in fact worldwide), it's reassuring to hear that mindfulness apps appear to be offering people one positive way of dealing with stress, anxiety and depression.

Next, being a very active person myself, I asked Craig what he feels are the most popular mindfulness activities.

The Science of Play

The most popular mindfulness activities

Statistically speaking, the following activities are the most common in mindfulness circles according to The Good Body website.

1: Meditation

» It is estimated that somewhere between 200 and 500 million people practise a form of meditation.

» In the United States approximately 14 per cent of adults have practised meditation at least once. In Australia, this figure is around 16 per cent.

» Meditation is almost as popular as yoga in the Unites States as a form of mind-body intervention (14.3 per cent as opposed to 14.2 per cent).

» The number of adults who practise meditation tripled over the eight years from 2011, while the practice among children aged 16 years and under increased by 1000 per cent.

» The Headspace meditation app has been downloaded over 40 million times since it was founded in 2010.

2: Yoga

» In the United States, participation in yoga increased from 9.5 per cent to 14.3 per cent in 2012–2017.

» In Australia, participation in yoga-related activity doubled from 2008 to 2016, making it the fastest growing sports or fitness activity.

» Yoga is now considered more mainstream due to major sporting stars and teams incorporating it into their weekly training schedules.

(continued)

> » Yoga has moved with demand and now offers traditional yoga alongside hybrid and speed versions using equipment.
>
> ### 3: Colouring books for adults
>
> » Adult colouring books have become so popular that they began being published commercially in 2012–2013. They:
>
>> » are easily customised to meet any market demographic
>>
>> » are shown to increase mindfulness
>>
>> » produce art that can be kept and viewed or stored as desired
>>
>> » are recognised as a form of accepted therapy
>>
>> » allow people to fulfil their inner child through colouring
>>
>> » can be used to frame social interactions
>>
>> » allow for an escape from the sometimes harsh realities of day-to-day life.
>
> » In Australia, the COVID-19 pandemic and associated isolation restrictions were seen as the reason for a surge in Google searches for adult colouring books in March/April 2020. IP addresses listed as being in Victoria, the state with the harshest lockdown policies, recorded the highest volume of searches.

As we have seen, mindfulness is (thankfully) growing in popularity across the world.

Truthfully, I find play helps me achieve the meaning of mindfulness that Craig describes better than popular practices of mindfulness such as meditation, yoga and colouring.

Professor Alison James confirms there's quite a strong link between the two (although there are also subtle differences between them).

The link between play and mindfulness

> **The Science of Play**

Play and mindfulness can both lead us to be completely in the moment, with no thought of anything beyond the present.

Hungarian psychologist Mihaly Csikszentmihalyi pioneered research into happiness and is renowned for his theory of 'flow', which is considered a sign of play at its best. We are in flow when we are totally absorbed in what we are doing — when time and the need to eat or drink have fallen away because we are 'in the zone'. A sense of effortlessness arises from the flow state: everything seems to come naturally and we don't have to try. Such a feeling might accompany both play and meditation, but not always.

Everyone has 'off days' when they can't quite get their play vibe going. We also have good days when we are playing at our very best. Meditation is the same: it can be a deeply calming and insightful process, or a time when we feel fidgety and distracted and possibly even a bit bored. This sense of performing at our peak is often associated with talent or mastery of something, like the ballerina who performs a triple pirouette or the guitar player who just has that feel for the strings, sound and rhythm. (We'll come back to this in a moment.)

So we can see there are strong parallels between mindfulness and play. However, there are also subtle differences between them.

First of all, our mental and physical state will both affect and depend on the kind of play we are involved in. To see this in action, let's look at two examples.

1. You are careering around the squash court in a friendly game against your brother, who you have never beaten, but are desperate to beat. Amazingly — for the first time *ever* — you are getting close to that final winning shot. Your energy levels, focus, drive and sense of purpose are

(continued)

adrenaline-charged and your heart is pumping. You don't even know how you are managing to dart around the court with such agility and speed because you are totally taken over by the sight of imminent victory.

2. You are on holidays, bathing in a crystal-clear lake on a sunny day, with the sun on your face and the mountains on the horizon. The water is warm and you have nowhere to be; you're just amusing yourself floating along with the gentle current, wondering how many times you can turn your body in circles by paddling with one hand.

Do one, both or neither of these play states seem mindful to you? Can you see parallels with aspects of flow? Is it tempting to say that the swimmer is closer to being mindful because of the sense of calm? In each case there is a play goal that you should direct your efforts towards and make in-the-moment judgements to achieve.

In mindfulness, however, the only goal is that of focusing on the breath and cultivating awareness by non-judgemental non-doing. Instead of harnessing and directing energy towards an end, the practice is about letting go and not striving for anything.

Another key difference relates to acceptance of the present moment and letting go. This is definitely not the squash player, and may not even be the swimmer, although the latter may be a lot closer. The swimmer will be seeking, however gently or urgently, to be in a flow state and to be present in order to achieve their aim.

In mindfulness, accepting the present moment and what we feel without trying to change it or judge it is the only goal. Of course, we can't avoid making judgements and having thoughts altogether — we are conditioned to do this. However, we note those judgements and allow them to move on, rather than holding onto or acting on them.

Another aspect of the similarity and/or difference between mindfulness and play relates to how we do it. Let's go back to our earlier thought about talent and mastery. We have identified the flow state as sometimes being associated with peak performance – although mindfulness is not a competitive sport! Nor is it about attaining any particular state, such as a trance, although other forms of meditation may lead to this. But both do involve practise.

Mindfulness experts such as Jon Kabat-Zinn, Mark Williams and Danny Penman all advocate practising mindfulness in order to use its techniques more effectively. It is the same with sport, music and other types of play. However, the word 'practice' is well chosen for another reason.

Yoga – as well as mindfulness – teachers refer to the combinations of stretches and poses as a practice because engaging in them is a never-ending journey. There is no final end point you are trying to get to because you can always learn and develop through what you do. What we desire is for our continued practice to help us make progress and get better. It may be subtle, it may be personal, but it is our progress. And this is another important factor that is common to mindfulness and play: both are entirely and freely at our disposal and it is up to us to determine how we want to benefit from them. Both are about getting back to the core of who we are and of our experience. Both allow us to enhance our human condition and how we live in and see the world.

I love these words from Alison. It's great to find a deeper understanding around what can act as a divider, or distinguisher, between play and mindfulness. My goal has always been about finding which play-based activities enable me to accomplish complete mindfulness. That means, exercising play that allows me (and those I work with) to fully 'let go'. Our games have no particular goal that's as important as feeling free, joyful and in the moment.

In my experience, being fully absorbed in play is the only way I've ever been able to achieve what I imagine is a total state of being 'in the moment' — with no external thoughts entering or disrupting my flow.

'Play-based mindfulness' helps describe this. It is a term I invented that's based on my own experience. When my life was not in a good place, the only time I could shut off my mind and be fully present was when I was playing in some form. Play allows time to stand completely still.

I do think the term 'mindfulness' gets used a lot (maybe too much) today, which can make its definition or meaning confusing. According to Craig Daly, there are more than 100 different meanings for mindfulness. Commonalities indicate a focus placed on attention, awareness and being present in (or returning to) the moment.

But there's a good reason it's growing in popularity and people are seeking 'mindful' states more than ever before.

My experience of what I believe to be mindfulness didn't happen through meditation or the practice of yoga, which isn't a bad thing, as those two activities aren't for everyone.

In my own mind, and through my own observations, mindfulness has taken on the meaning of being able to close off your mind and control your thoughts for even a small, special period of time. It's in this time that you are your most present. Where the past is not eating away at your soul, and the future is not giving you anxiety or causing you to feel feelings of fear or angst.

When I first started experimenting with different forms of mindfulness I found that it was similar to play. As with play, we don't always know that we are in a flow state. There may be certain routines and activities you do where you are present and in the moment but not aware of it.

I have found using the following self-assessment checklist helps. Give it a try for yourself.

A quick self-assessment: Are you 'all work'?

	Yes/No?
I often struggle with 'being present'.	
I often put in 'extra hours' at the office, or for work, when I am not really required or asked to.	
I often lose out on sleep because my mind is ticking over, trying to solve the next day's problems.	
I get paranoid about work, or let work-related problems consume me.	
In social situations, I often feel uneasy and like I need to check in on work, on my phone or on emails.	
I have seen relationships break down or disintegrate due to my work.	
I find it very difficult to 'shut off' and shut my brain down.	

If you answered 'yes' to any of these questions, I strongly recommend practising mindfulness in some way, shape or form. If you find it difficult to meditate, practise deep breathing or yoga or (like me) just try playing. It could be something simple like kicking a footy with a relative, playing a card game (maybe that's where '500' can come in handy!), getting out a musical instrument or spending as little as five minutes on the floor, rolling about or throwing a ball to your pet. Whatever helps you get in the moment and find your calm.

Last, but not least

1.   Mindfulness comes in all shapes and
     forms, much as play does. It can mean
     different things to different people – and
     that's all right. This explains why there
     are so many different definitions for
     mindfulness.

2.   The power and beauty of being present and still in the
     moment is something we all need and secretly crave
     in our busy, crazy world. For me, play is the way to
     find stillness and to stop my thoughts of the past and
     the future. It allows me to be 100 per cent focused on
     everything around me in the present.

3.   If you are yet to find what mindfulness looks and feels
     like for you, I urge you to keep searching, exploring
     and trying new things. Your mindfulness might be just
     around the corner. Some people search their entire lives
     to find their purpose, career and passion. Others know
     it straight away. It's the same with mindfulness: it may
     come easily to some and not to others, and it may come
     when you're 10 years old or 110 years old.

part II

the PROOF behind PLAY

Chapter 6
Our brain during play

IT'S INTERESTING TO CONSIDER what happens to our brain when we play, and what, undoubtedly, happens to it when we don't play enough. As with defining and categorising 'play', explaining exactly what happens to our brain when we're playing — and, subsequently, having fun — is extremely difficult. I can only describe the upside of play on our brains through my own experiences.

But first, I'll try to capture it through a more 'research-y' lens.

In the article 'Lighten up — according to science, it's good for you', published online by *Johns Hopkins Magazine* in 2016, writer Julie Scharper talks about 'fun' — that elated feeling we have when we play — as 'vague' and 'highly subjective'.

According to Scharper, neuroscience professor David J Linden maintains that fun is 'not a term that scientists use'. However, Scharper says, Linden is well informed on the subject of pleasure, a concept closely related to fun. In his book, *The Compass of Pleasure,* he describes how participating in activities as varied as drug use, sex, exercise and altruism can affect the brain in similar ways.

Linden explains that when people feel pleasure, neurons activate in the ventral tegmental area of the brain. According to Scharper's article, 'The long, spindly axons of these neurons reach into other parts of the brain as the roots of one tree wrap around those of another. When the neuron fires, the ends of the axons release the neurotransmitter dopamine [a 'chemical messenger' found in our body that plays a critical role in how we feel pleasure], which is then absorbed by neurons in other regions of the brain.'

And it's this pleasure pathway, says Linda Gorman, teaching professor at the Krieger School's Neuroscience Program, that rewards behaviour, which benefits the survival of both individuals and species.

In other words, engaging in 'fun' — or leisurely activities — helps us release dopamine. And when we feel pleasure, our 'pleasure pathway' is activated, rewarding our behaviour, which is beneficial to our survival. But how does this actually work?

Professor Linden explains the process, using exercise as an example. Exercise stimulates the pleasure pathways not only in humans, but also in rats and mice: 'A rat will press a lever a hundred times to access a running wheel.'

The 'feeling of euphoria', says Scharper, 'after a long run, is triggered by ... endorphins flooding the brain.'

Scharper goes on to say that laboratory mice appear to take great delight in playing on running wheels. They can run on a wheel for as long as 18 minutes, some even hanging onto it after running as if they were on a merry-go-round. And they have been observed accessing hamster wheels 'like miniature fitness buffs' without being lured by food.

Scharper continues by saying that 'Natural selection would seem to favour animals and humans who get a buzz out of chasing prey or running away from predators.'

So, having fun and stimulating our neural pathways is beneficial to our survival. But why do we enjoy participating in fun and enjoyable activities that have no obvious tie to our survival?

Professor Linden describes what happens in humans as 'a miracle'. 'Not only can humans take pleasure from things that have no relation to getting genes to the next generation, but we can take pleasure from things like fasting and celibacy, acts that run counter to the evolutionary imperative.'

Scharper concludes that 'Perhaps these pleasurable activities could all be seen as a form of play. And play might just be the most important act we can engage in.'

According to an article on the HelpGuide website titled 'The benefits of play for adults', there are myriad benefits of play, not only for children, but for adults too.

The article states that play helps to:

» *relieve stress*. Play can trigger the release of endorphins, which make us feel good and can temporarily relieve pain.

» *improve brain function*. Play helps to prevent memory problems and ward off stress and depression.

» *stimulate the mind and boost creativity*. We learn new tasks more easily when they are fun and we're in a relaxed and playful mood. Play can also stimulate our imagination, helping us to adjust to and solve problems.

» *improve relationships and our connection to others*. By sharing laughter and fun we foster empathy, compassion, trust and intimacy with others. Play doesn't have to include a specific activity; it can be simply a state of mind.

» *keep you feeling young and energetic*. George Bernard Shaw said, 'We don't stop playing because we grow old; we grow old because we stop playing'. By boosting our energy and vitality and improving our resistance to disease, play helps us function at our best.

Personally, I have seen the benefits of play in helping shift my thought patterns and perspective on activities I'm undertaking or in relation to the world around me.

Each year, I have the pleasure of working alongside several different sporting clubs as they undertake pre-season training.

For example, I've worked with the Frankston Dolphins men's and women's senior AFL sides (a sporting club located south-east of Melbourne's CBD in Victoria, Australia). Pre-season can be extremely hard, not a lot of fun and extremely repetitive. Competition (paid) sport is sometimes a job and we don't always find work that enjoyable!

Being someone who has played organised sport at quite a senior level, I remember dreading pre-season. Typically, it would involve countless sprints up and down a field. We'd do a couple of hundred push-ups (which after a break felt extremely tough). And to top it off, pre-season for most sports, particularly Australian Rules Football, usually takes place in summer under our hot, Australian sun. Sound like fun? I can tell you, your brain definitely doesn't find it fun at the time.

Going back to clubs as a trainer, I've noticed that the pre-season and its drills haven't really changed much. The methods of regaining fitness and optimising your player skillsets are pretty much the same. You have the same old sprints, push-ups and one hell of a voice inside your head hating on your body (or your trainer!).

This is a structure that, as a fitness coach, I also have to follow. The only difference is that I approach these drills using 'play' as a tactic, which makes the players work harder because they're having more fun while doing them.

I've found that by introducing play, fun and laughter into what is often a serious and gruelling collection of drills, our brains help our body to train harder because mentally we begin resisting the exercises far less.

Play has taught me that regardless of what you're doing (even if it's physically pushing your body to the limit in pre-season training), if you add something simple, like a couple of dice or a bit of silliness to the movement or you ramp up some friendly competition, your brain's thought patterns often instantly change.

Instead of counting down the number of reps you're doing and stressing over how many you have left, when you add a playful element into the drill, it becomes a game and you're more inclined to enjoy it.

For example, I like to separate individuals into teams when we do repetitive sprints and runs. Suddenly, you're not just sprinting and running for yourself — you're sprinting and running for others too. Then, instead of simply counting down the reps: '100, 99, 98, 97 — 97 more left , guys! Keep going!', I add up individual reps and count them as 'points' that then go towards a team's score. Through play, I've found I've been able to help pre-season footy (and other sports) players enjoy their drills (a tad more!) instead of absolutely dreading each and every session.

Another example of how play can change our mindset is my personal account of giving a TEDx Talk.

While I'm used to speaking for hours on end with people from all across the globe, TEDx is one platform that (while I was extremely excited to do it) scared the hell out of me. Yes, I am a confident speaker. But I'm used to a fairly flexible format that allows me to go off on tangents and then eventually rein myself back in!

The TEDx Talk program (which is a grassroots initiative that allows communities to discover 'ideas worth sharing') expects speakers to talk for 15 minutes and 15 minutes only. That constraint really worried me and made me feel apprehensive right up until I was on stage. But I had made a considered decision early on that if I was going to do a good job on stage, I had to break the ice early, build connections with the audience and make myself feel at ease up there. So, despite people telling me ahead of time I shouldn't play a game with the audience, that's exactly what I did.

I had resolved to help make myself comfortable and confident in my abilities as a speaker by starting off with an interactive game (between myself and the audience).

You can watch hundreds of TED, or TEDx, Talks and I don't think you'll stumble across anyone who has started off with a game. But this is a proven method I use to begin every meeting, speech, workshop or keynote. I didn't see why speaking on the red circle at TEDx should be any different. So, I started it off with a game to not only help make me, but also the audience, feel far more comfortable and in the present moment.

In this TEDx Talk[3], I exercised the power of play in a few different ways.

Firstly, as the speaker, it helped me to feel more in my element. It also centred me in the moment and heightened my feelings of being present and connected with my audience.

Secondly, for the audience, playing a three-minute game before settling in to watch a TEDx Talk was something completely unexpected and novel. It was three minutes of joy and laughter that helped boost their energy levels and make them feel ready to take on board what I was about to present to them.

In this instance, play allowed me to change the audience's thought process in a way that was advantageous to me and my keynote on the day.

Before we move on to talking about our mood when we play, I'd like to share another story from Dr Craig Daly, in which he reflects on the mental changes he experienced during a hard fun run, where he encountered 'Sato-san'.

----

[3] **Follow this QR code to see my TEDx Talk.**

The wisdom of Sato-san

The term 'fun run' is often referred to as an oxymoron, that being the conjunction of contradictory terms in a figure of speech.

It was May 1996 and I, fast approaching 35 years of age, had decided to test my aerobic endurance by entering a specific fun run, the Brisbane Half Marathon. For some obscure reasons, the age of 35 for me heralded the commencement of middle age. I figured by testing myself physically, and succeeding, I could somehow postpone this symbolic journey. While I had completed plenty of 10k fun runs previously, I was now venturing into a running unknown by completing 21.0975 kilometres in a target time of 1:45:00; just on the five minutes per kilometre pace I could comfortably run at. Not fast by running standards, but respectable I thought.

It had been some five years since I had retired as a weathered but still competitive first-grade hockey player, yet my job as a physical education teacher at a large primary school, my 5–8-kilometre afternoon runs through the Burleigh Heads National Park and the weekly social game of touch football kept me in reasonable shape. No other training was contemplated. Messages from colleagues who were more seasoned runners regarding the possible pitfalls of my approach were dismissed. I would be fine, I told them. I was wrong.

The only positive I could draw on for the day's efforts was that I finished. More accurately, it finished me. I was travelling well until the 10-kilometre mark. Then, slowly but surely, the lack of preparation kicked in. Each passing kilometre took longer and my target time approached, arrived and disappeared into the abyss. The last two kilometres involved a movement not unlike the Cliff Young shuffle, somewhat accentuated by a chafing on my inner thighs not seen since my days as a rotund toddler. I crossed the finish line at the same time as a group of power walkers, in a very leisurely 2:15:00. Collecting both my finisher's medal and T-shirt, I found a place to lie down.

Disheartened, dehydrated and distraught with the result, but somehow determined that it wouldn't define me.

I immediately set my goal of completing the Gold Coast Half Marathon in early July, some seven weeks away. After a week of well-needed rest, and armed with more suitable longer run research, I started again. I trained like I had never trained before. My regular 5–8-kilometre runs were stretched to 10–12 kilometres. My partner and I taught at the same school, some 15 kilometres from our home. Twice a week, before 6 am, I would set off early and run on our usual route to school, and she would pick me up around the 13-kilometre mark. Each run became easier as I focused not on the race, but on the surroundings. I became grateful for the time and opportunities I had to train. Time in front of the television was spent either stretching, or rolling out aches and pains in the quads and hamstrings. By the time July came round I was ready. My target time of 1:45:00 seemed achievable.

Race day dawned clear. Southerners would say we don't really have winter on the Gold Coast, but the garbage bag I had over my torso, and the crowd of people massing together near the starting line kept the coolish temperature from my mind. It was then I saw him. Standing by himself, a small Asian man, dressed in a red-and-white running singlet, with a cap proudly displaying the Japanese flag. He was smiling, laughing and holding his hand high, no doubt in the hope of a high five from anyone in his general vicinity. His good intentions were obviously lost on those around him, for he received nothing back.

I had no-one else to talk to, so I ventured over, gave him a high five, and we started to talk. His name was Sato-san, and in broken English, he told me that this would be his 55th half marathon in his 63 years on the planet. He had run races in all parts of the world, but the Gold Coast race was his favourite. He was hoping to break his personal best of 1:30:00 minutes.

I was in awe. I wondered how the small, sinewy legs had carried him so far, so quickly and so often. When I asked him for his training secret he simply replied: 'me never stop'. For some

(continued)

30 minutes, he talked of his love of running, of travelling to different countries, of meeting people and of sharing goodwill. He said his favourite part was waiting at the start for others to go ahead, and then offering his good fortune to all as he went past. I told him of my previous effort in Brisbane, and how I was using that as motivation for a better finish this time. His response struck at my soul.

'Craig-san, you should run with love, not with spite. World too good a place not to enjoy freedom running bring. Many people never know joy running bring. You never stop.'

I thanked him for his advice, wished him well and headed to the start line. Run with love? I wasn't really sure what he meant.

The race started and I somehow managed to attach myself to a fast-moving pack early on. Running with others was always my preferred option. This way I had people to talk with to disrupt the monotony of one step after the other, and to motivate me to keep going. Without friends to run with I needed to attach to somebody.

However, punching through the five-kilometre mark in a tick under 20 minutes, it became obvious that this was the wrong group to be with. By the eight-kilometre mark I was working far harder than I wanted to stay in touch, and I began to drop off. The well-intentioned motivational taunts were only in earshot for a short while as the pack surged ahead. Some two kilometres later, I crashed. Despite my increased training, the early pace had taken its toll, and as the pain in my legs increased, the demons from Brisbane resurfaced — and they were angry. I pulled to the side of the road, found a place to sit on the kerb and wasted time under the pretence of fixing my running shoe.

As I wrestled with the physical and psychological barriers, my new-found friend from earlier reappeared. Sato-san looked like he was out on a morning stroll, so easily was he travelling, with a wide smile under his Japanese cap. Seeing my difficulties in moving from my now very comfortable position, he rallied a cry of 'Ganbatte-ne, Craig-san'! Roughly translated — 'you can do this'. He grabbed my arm and assisted me back onto the road. 'We run with love,' he said, over and over again.

Despite my pain, his actions had an immediate effect on me. The doubt that had enveloped me some five minutes earlier was now gone. My breathing returned to normal, my stride now more fluent, and my pace back to that of someone who had trained for the event. After a short time running together, with me meeting his relaxed rhythm, he looked down at his watch, patted my back and then he was gone. His rapid departure left me alone physically, but I began to appreciate the morning in its entirety. I smelled the fresh Gold Coast air, marvelled at the coastal landscape and gave thanks for the continual cheers from the spectators dotting the route to the finish line. You might say I was running with love.

As I approached the finish chute I saw him again. He stood by the final turn, with his finisher's medal glistening prominently in the morning sunlight, cheering every runner to the finish line. When he saw me he raised both his hands in the sky, and then bowed. When I crossed the line I looked up to the finishing clock to see the elapsed time — 1:36:09. I had made it. As I stumbled across the line I dissolved into a river of tears. Happy that I had met my goal, but somewhat sad that my finishing time meant so much to me. The lessons learned during the last nine kilometres had momentarily disappeared.

It took a while to find Sato-san after the race. I wanted ... no, I needed to thank him for his guidance and his kindness. It took some time but I found him near the inflatable Gatorade bottle, surrounded by a crowd of other runners, all offering their congratulations. It became obvious I wasn't the only one he had helped that morning. He saw me from a distance. 'Craig-san! You finish. Congratulations.' I smiled, clapped my hands, bowed and left him to the others. He had given me enough.

Run with love. Almost 25 years have passed and I still remember Sato-san. My health battles over the past five years have highlighted the importance of his message. Now, even though I'm approaching 60, mostly retired and with a suspect back and dodgy knees, I no longer run far at all. Those days are gone. I am older, slower and more out of shape than my younger version, but I remain resolute. I covet the chance to exercise on a regular basis. Yet, despite having ample time, my goal of

(continued)

> 15 000 steps a day, combined with some form of stretching and/
> or swimming, is never an easy one to complete. Occasionally,
> travelling and consultancy commitments, the completion of
> home duties and/or apathy see me fall well short, but never two
> days in succession. If I'm ever unsure, I think back to 1996 — to a
> 63-year-old Japanese man who made running look so, so easy. I
> can still hear his cry of 'Ganbatte-ne, Craig-san! Run with love.'
> You can do this! And so I do. Me never stop.

We would all love to have a Sato-san in our lives every day. Someone
to tell us, 'You've got this!' when we think we haven't. But, as we've
seen, there are ways we can shift our mindset by including play
in our daily activities — and it's something we can easily achieve
without anyone else's encouragement.

Boosting our mood

Play can be a brilliant way to instantly enhance your mood
either momentarily or more consistently, if you ritualise it in your
daily routine.

One thing I notice when I speak to large workplaces full of stressed-
out employees, or in schools, is that the keynotes always tend to
schedule me at the end of the day when everyone's tired, worn out
and not in the mood. The last thing they want to see is me rock up
with a smile on my face and a lot of energy — worst of all, expecting
them to be in the same mindset as I am.

I couldn't count the number of times CEOs, directors, principals
and coaches have gone out of their way in the lead-up to sessions
to tell me that they don't like team building and hate icebreakers.
And I totally get this. I'm sure we have all had a bad experience

with 'icebreakers' (myself included), where we're forced to stand in a circle and everyone has to take it in turn to say their name and share something about themselves. I call these types of activities 'ice makers' because they tend to make everyone nervous and self-conscious.

Instead of people listening and learning about their peers, activities like these make them focus inwards, to think solely about what they're going to say. It's only when their turn is over that they feel some kind of reprieve and become more present in the moment. These activities are quite uninventive and often plain awkward.

I believe a good icebreaker or team-building game is one that doesn't shine the light on just one person.

People need to feel safe and confident they can express themselves freely without being judged. So, I believe a good icebreaker or team-building game is one where everyone is able to fully engage in what it is they are doing, without feeling worried about what those around them are thinking. Instead of calling these group activities 'icebreakers' or 'team-building exercises' I call them 'connection starters'. In part IV of the book I share instructions on how to play four of the connection starters I use with groups and individuals. They are 'One, Two, Three', 'Three Is a Charm', 'Clapping: 1, 2, 3' and 'Drawing Animals on Your Head'.

In the first 20 minutes of starting a workshop, I usually play three or four 'connection starters' with the room, and instantly the atmosphere feels more positive.

We've seen in previous chapters that play-based activities can also serve to help people be more 'in the moment' and worry less about the stressful, high-pressure situations they get caught up in on a daily basis. They also create a space and environment where being vulnerable, curious and innovative are encouraged and promoted by all.

When play is incorporated into the workplace, at home or at school the right way, it helps us connect and build stronger, more trusting relationships with one another. This means our mood becomes more positive, which helps us to feel safe and comfortable.

Last, but not least

1. When we are play-deprived it's like abusing our brains and body. It has a similar effect to what sleep deprivation has on our body and mind in terms of alertness and decision making.

2. If we haven't enjoyed play for years, we can become joyless, lose our curiosity or become workaholics. It's like not having our morning coffee — we all know that feeling! Reintroducing play to our lives is a massive opportunity to change our ways and add joy, fun, connection and energy to our brain and mood.

3. I think deep down we all have a Sato-san in our lives — we just might not realise who it is. Take a moment to reflect on who could be the Sato-san in your life.

4. Being a leader and building powerful connections is something you have the opportunity to do every day. We've seen how play can build connections and inject fun into work and life. How do you create a safe and inclusive environment wherever you are?

Chapter 7

The power of play

LIKE MANY, I THINK one of the best ways to grow, develop and experience life in all its beauty is through travel. Whether it's around your own country and backyard, or overseas.

In my life, I have been extremely fortunate to visit a lot of incredible places around the world and I've witnessed the impact of play on a global scale.

In my early twenties, I lived and worked in London (as a teacher). And it was from the UK that I went on several trips around Europe, the USA and the African continent. Every time I visited somewhere new, I would make it my mission to mix and mingle with the locals. And one of the best ways I know to do this is through the power of sport — in this case, soccer (or football, as it's called in many countries).

Soccer helped me to connect with people I might otherwise not have been able to communicate with. It was interesting to observe how countries had different ways of playing soccer: from the ball they used to the size of the 'soccer field'. And each country had a slightly different set of rules to suit their style of game.

This is what I truly believe play is all about. You can mix and mould play so you get the most pleasure out of it. And, much like soccer, it takes on a universality like no other activity.

To help describe the power of play that I observed during my travels around the globe I've selected examples of the sport in action from a few of the places I visited.

An 'ANZAC clash' in Turkey

I was in Turkey on the cusp of the 150th anniversary of the ANZACs at Gallipoli. The purpose of our trip was to witness the dawn service at ANZAC Cove and pay tribute to the brave soldiers who had gone to battle all those years ago. I was in the company of a lot of other Australians, and together we created a soccer team and played an 'ANZAC clash' against a group of local Turks.

We played our match on a traditional rectangular pitch with a standard round ball. It was a great match (though not overly competitive). Everyone appeared to enjoy each other's company and after the game, we spent the evening together as a group — eating, drinking, laughing and sharing stories. It was the soccer game that allowed us to connect and create common ground. It broke down language barriers and was an important connector for building up rapport, trust and comradery.

Soccer on the bank of the Nile

While I was on a tour in Egypt with friends, we spent two nights sailing down the Nile on a felucca, which is a wooden sailing boat somewhat like a giant bamboo raft. This was an incredible and memorable trip, and I remember loving every second of it. Except for one thing.

Being white Australian males, my friend Jonny and I felt that people (particularly the locals) instantly assumed we were wealthy and began to treat us differently from the others. Egypt isn't alone in this — it's something a lot of white men can relate to in many parts of the world, particularly where money is harder to come by. However, we made a strong effort to connect with the locals through play.

On the second night, we pulled up on the bank of the Nile to dock for the night. Soon after, three workers and the captain took a plastic, 1.25-litre Coke bottle onto shore and began playing soccer on the sandbank against another team of crew members. This captured my attention and cemented the notion that you really can play soccer anywhere, and with anything, if you really try! Naturally, being the sports-inclined person I am, I wanted to join in. So, Jonny and I walked over and asked the local teams if we could play as well. Without a second thought and with beaming smiles, they separated us and directed each of us to join one team.

For that 30 or 40 minutes, we were all equal. And it was the only time during the trip that they didn't bow or stop to do something for us. We played hard, had fun and laughed together.

Play allows people from all walks of life to be equal. It is the ultimate way to level the playing field because play doesn't, and shouldn't, discriminate. Otherwise, it isn't play.

The language of soccer

It was in Malawi that I again observed the power of play in action — acting as a means of communication for people from opposite walks of life without a common verbal language.

Malawi is a landlocked country in south-eastern Africa and is among the poorest countries in the world. I remember driving on the roads and being surprised by the lack of cars. You can drive 20 to 30 minutes and not see another vehicle. The locals walk or occasionally get around by bicycle.

Malawi is one of the few poorer countries I have visited where children and families (often mothers) don't ask you for money as you pass by but for the clothes off your back or shoes off your feet. For them, these materials are hard to come by and they aren't something a small amount of change can easily buy.

Despite the impoverished circumstances, I will never forget how happy the general population of Malawi appeared to be. I can honestly say they are one of the happiest communities I've ever witnessed.

One day, I watched a group of 15 youths ranging in age from eight to 15 years playing an intense game of soccer outside the campground I was staying at. The soccer pitch was a tiny patch of red dirt alongside a road. They didn't have straight goals (they had erected bits of bent wood), no-one was wearing shoes and they were kicking around a soccer ball crafted from bits of rubbish. The youths had squashed a couple of plastic bottles and used plastic and rubber bands to mould the materials into a round-shaped ball. It was a stark reminder that no matter where you are — or what materials and tools you have access to — you can literally create a game out of, or play with, anything.

Once I had recognised this as a version of soccer, I walked over to the group in the hope of joining in. When I asked them if I could join their game, the kids stopped playing and stared at me. I quickly realised my English (and ocker Australian accent) was lost on them. So I made a kicking movement with my foot and pointed to the ball and then at my chest. Unanimously, they started smiling and clapping, asked me to remove my shoes and pointed out the direction in which I was to kick (if I wanted to score a goal). We couldn't understand each other by communicating verbally, but we played and enjoyed each other's company for more than an hour before I had to stop because my feet were bleeding!

The following morning, as our tour bus was departing the campgrounds, I watched as five of the boys I had played soccer with ran alongside the bus, smiling at me while waving and laughing. They were wearing the clothes I had gifted them after our match, which filled me with a real sense of gratitude for the experience we had shared.

Those clothes had never afforded me any particular joy, but for these boys they were something from my life they could keep forever — all thanks to a game of soccer.

Connecting in Machu Picchu

The final story I'd like to share with you is about my time in Machu Picchu.

Machu Picchu is a 15th century Inca trail located in southern Peru, South America. It is one of the original seven natural wonders of the world. Trekking Machu Picchu was an amazing experience, made even better by the company I kept.

On the four-day hike, I met people of all ages from Australia, New Zealand, South Africa, Canada and the United States. In true Dale fashion, I wanted to form connections among the groups by initiating a game or by means of a connection starter.

I decided the simplest game was 'Rock, Paper, Scissors'. Now, this is a great game because it relies predominantly on luck, not skill, meaning there are fewer barriers to winning. It also doesn't require detailed instructions, which is great when you're looking to play with people from a variety of backgrounds and countries ... but I wanted to take the game to the next level.

Have you ever played 'Evolution'? Here's the gist of the game.

'Evolution'

Number of players

10 to 1000 (the more players, the better)

How the game is played

Each participant starts as an 'egg'. They are told to make the sound (nice and loud) that an egg makes.

Yes, it's ridiculous. And funny because people make up random noises since — let's be honest — no-one knows what sound an egg makes!

To start the game, two eggs play 'Rock, Paper, Scissors' against each other. The winner then turns into a 'chicken', and the loser stays as an egg.

The losing egg has to play off against another egg while the chicken has to make the sound of a chicken before playing off against the same of their kind.

When two chickens play each other, the winner turns into a 'monster' who then has to make a monster sound. But the loser (the chicken) becomes an egg again.

Confused? Don't fret! Here is a video[4] of us playing 'Evolution' in Peru.

[4] **Follow this QR code to watch us play 'Evolution'.**

The game essentially works by allowing winners to move up the food chain, while the losers continue to drop down the chain.

The game should always finish when one person turns into a 'human' (after two monsters challenge off) and the winner makes it to the top of the food chain.

In truth, this game isn't about winning or losing. It's simply about making everyone feel comfortable being silly — making ridiculous noises — and gaming off against each other in a light-hearted way. I always find this game has people laughing at the end. In Machu Picchu, even those who looked sceptical at first started high-fiving other group members and looked like they could accomplish the trek in three days (not four).

This four-day trek ended up being a play-filled adventure for everyone.

After the first day of playing 'Evolution', the group leaders would call me out every morning to play something new so everyone could get pumped up and enthusiastic about the hike ahead. It was brilliant to observe. Especially when other groups at our campgrounds started to venture to our morning play sessions. Eventually, more and more game-seekers started to join in, and before too long we were no longer a group of predominately Aussies, New Zealanders, Canadians and Americans, but we were in the company of several different European nationalities as well.

On the last morning before we packed up our tents for the final time, we played 'Evolution' with the massive crowd we had attracted — not only the travellers who had joined in, but also five other groups (apart from ours) that wanted to participate, as well as our porters (who had helped carry our equipment and food up the trail).

This is the power of play. We had more than 10 different nationalities involved in this game, laughing unanimously, making silly sounds and connecting with one another. I don't think everyone fully understood how to play the game, but that didn't matter. If they were unsure, they modified it and found ways to make it work.

Simple games such as 'Evolution' were also great for forming interactions between people during the hike. At each stop, people would make chicken sounds and flap their arms when they saw me passing. A couple of the people in my group on the tour said that the morning games became a highlight of the trip. They couldn't remember the last time they had laughed so childishly and enjoyed themselves as much as they did through these connection starters.

❄ ❄ ❄

Put simply, play helps us dig deep into what really matters, forming meaningful connections with people we know, as well as complete strangers. Play helps us feel safe and part of a community. And most importantly, it helps us experience life to the absolute fullest. No matter where you are in the world, play is a uniting force.

Play is how we are accepted and welcomed into any tribe. When we reflect on its broader effect on our lives, we see that play enables bonds and relationships to blossom that might not have otherwise developed.

Our lives are better and brighter when we play with our family, in our workplace and with our friends — and even with strangers, as the stories you've just read demonstrate.

Last, but not least

1. Play has no boundaries, barriers, language or currency. It is accepted everywhere you go with a smile and is judgement free.

2. In a world where we crave and desire everything flash, new and fast, play offers a refreshing contrast. Play works best when you don't use the latest gadgets because the less you have, the more creative you need to be. Sometimes the joy is in the creative process where you create the equipment, the rules and the scoring system.

3. Travel is one of the best forms of education anyone can ever have. It doesn't matter if that's exploring your own country or others around the world.

4. Some of my most rewarding and memorable experiences are of travelling overseas — and of playing 'Connect Four' in Thailand, 'Giant Jenga' in Bali and 'Darts' in Ireland. What memories do you have where play was at the forefront of an experience? What where you doing, who were you with and how did this make you feel?

part III

the
BENEFITS
of PLAY

Chapter 8

Less work, more play

I'VE MENTIONED ALREADY HOW reconnecting with play and my inner-child — and departing an 'all work' mentality — was the first step I took to regaining joy and happiness in my life. After hitting rock bottom, and a really bad time, play permitted me to have short periods of refuge and calm, and it silenced my racing mind. It also enabled me to learn to smile, laugh and have fun with students I was teaching during my darkest hours. And this resulted in truly strong relationships forming between us.

Naturally, I never told the students I was teaching what was going on in my life, but I suspect they could tell I wasn't in a good place. On one occasion when I was feeling extremely low, I had to leave the room crying. It was the last day of term, and I had promised the cohort we would play a big game of footy (Australian Rules Football) on the oval to finish off the school term. But I just couldn't get myself to a place where I could face them.

Instead, I sat outside the classroom on my own.

Now, you could imagine kids of a certain age acting up and having slight disregard for their teachers. But to their credit, all the kids I taught could tell I was hurting. Instead of rushing out to the oval, they stayed in our classroom, cleaning and tidying up until it was spotless (something I had been nagging them to do all year!).

When the bell rang and the students had cleared out, I made my way back to the classroom to find a note on one of the front desks acknowledging that they could see I was upset. The note said they hoped a clean classroom would put a smile back on my face.

Now, I know this isn't specifically about play, but due to the relationships that play-based activities had allowed me to form with my students during the tough times in my life, it's something I thought I'd share. I didn't always see eye to eye with my students, nor did they with me. But they could read me and cared about me, and I cared about them too.

I found myself in situations like this more and more often, until I finally recognised how mandatory it was becoming for me to live my life's balance focusing more on play than work.

And that was the turning point for me — the beginning of a life of less work and more play.

Last, but not least

1. I've deliberately started part III of the book with a short, punchy chapter to highlight one of the single greatest gestures we have the power of fostering — namely, that we should never underestimate what a random act or simple gesture of kindness can do for someone's day, week or year.

2. Kindness — whether spoken or written — doesn't have to cost anything. It is a super power that we should all use often.

3. When was the last time you did something to make someone's day better — maybe a random act of kindness for stranger? Here's a challenge: next time you buy a takeaway coffee, pay for yours and ask the barista to take money for another coffee to give to someone for a free coffee. I like to pay it forward like this at least once a month — it puts a smile on my face knowing someone's morning will be brighter for it.

Chapter 9
Play for individuals, couples and families

IF WE THINK BACK to the last time we were doing something we loved, I can just about 100 per cent guarantee it involved some sort of play.

The benefits of play for individuals

Play is how we create memories and feel joy, which can be extremely beneficial to our individual wellbeing and mental health, particularly during challenging and unprecedented times.

I believe that right now the world's mental health is in a vulnerable state. It is estimated that one billion global citizens experience mental health issues at some stage of their lives or grapple with some form of ongoing mental health challenges.

Life is not always pleasant. It can be tough. So we need to do our best to find glimpses of fun, laughter and excitement — even when things are bad.

Here in Australia, for instance, 2020 threw us a global pandemic shortly after our country had been hit by mass bushfires. During this time, play was critical.

COVID-19 resulted in a national buzz around playful activities (particularly for adults). It became difficult to find popular games and activities that weren't sold out in stores and online. For a while, it seemed you couldn't purchase a bicycle anywhere and puzzles were as rare as hen's teeth.

I imagine play-based activities were in high demand not just here, but around the world. From painting kits, drawing sets and pottery kits to do-it-yourself cooking sets and classes, in times of chaos and angst, we search for new ways to spark joy and happiness in our daily lives.

Yes, we had more time than ever while stuck at home — particularly in Victoria. But it was a gift to some, who felt they had been granted a moment in time (however forced) to really step back, analyse their stressful and busy lives and get back to basics. Back to things that bring about true happiness and pleasure.

I hope this continues because when I started to put a lot of energy into improving my mood and focusing on my internal happiness, I began to see all aspects of my life improve. Think how happy our society would be if we all took the time to play. We'd feel younger and more energetic. And we'd be more positive within ourselves, which would naturally impact others positively.

The benefits of play for couples

Play is a fun and novel way to make relationships exciting and fresh. It helps keep the fun, laughter and passion alive between couples — all essential elements of a positive and healthy relationship.

In my own experiences of dating, or being in a relationship, play has been a powerful tool for helping us connect on a deeper, more meaningful level.

My lovely (now) wife Bree is going to get a mention in the following story — which she probably won't like. But it's important for me to share my personal experiences of how play can benefit relationships.

No doubt you've heard of the dating app Tinder. This app has inbuilt gamifying elements. You swipe left or right to find a match with someone you feel you'll be suited to or are attracted to.

Well, when I used Tinder (after my divorce and before meeting Bree), I often found that the app itself was the most fun and playful part of the dating experience. To me, dates that involved going out for drinks or dinner were dull and boring

So I used to make a conscious effort to really mix it up. I would suggest going ten-pin bowling, walking, going to the driving range and playing mini golf. And if a date did take place in a bar, I'd make sure there was a game such as 'Connect Four' or 'Jenga' for us to play.

Bringing play-based activities into your dating life is, I believe, extremely advantageous. You get to see people's real emotions, feelings and qualities a lot more quickly. You discover what type of competitor they are, or how they deal with winning and losing. You also learn what kind of negotiating style they have. These are all qualities that become important when you're in a relationship.

When I met Bree, we had our second date at a bar. One of the first things I spotted was the 'Connect Four' game — the centuries old game that I believe Captain Cook may have played on his long voyages of discovery.

Can you believe that we played 'Connect Four' for four hours that night? It gave us so much joy. It was a light-hearted and competitive activity. And it was a great way to start getting more comfortable with each other without having to talk the whole time.

On our third date we went ten-pin bowling. This is where the fun, loving and competitive side of my now wife really came out.

Don't get me wrong — talking is great. And you definitely need to be able to sit and talk with your partner, both in a serious and a non-serious manner. But early on in a relationship, play is a brilliant way to make your time together feel unique.

Injecting play-based activities into the time you spend together (and ensuring you both see them as 'play' and as enjoyable) stops your time together from getting boring or stale (which is often inevitable). Play is a great way to ensure you'll experience a lot more highs together, especially when we know (as adults) times can get tough, stressful and complex.

As I said before, Bree and I are married now. I'm sure it won't surprise you to know we have games in every corner of the house. We also have two different types of 'Connect Four'. This game evokes special memories for us and each time we play, it's as exciting as the last time.

The benefits of play for families

Families are built around play. Play helps us improve our social skills. It teaches us to cooperate and can be a great tool to help heal resentment and hurt after arguments or disagreements.

Think of families as you would a sporting team. To succeed as a family, we need to be unified and work together, have trust in one another and communicate.

Play helps improve our communication. It helps us form deeper connections and love in our relationships, and at times when we feel our 'team' is 'losing', play can help families work together towards a common goal and output — in other words, to feel like winners. When our family environment feels positive, everyone is healthy, safe and living in harmony.

I often reflect on the lessons I learned through play as I was growing up.

At the start of this book, I talked about the developmental learning I received from playing LEGO with my two younger sisters. I spoke of the benefits of building cubbies, climbing trees and playing with children of various ages.

As a kid, play taught me not only how to be a good winner, but also a good loser. As adults we may no longer need the developmental learning that play provides, but it can assist us by helping relieve stress and making us a more pleasant family member to be around.

It can help us feel grounded in the moment, and to break down barriers so that we connect better with those around us — whether they are our children, our partner, our siblings, our parents or our extended family.

My family grew up playing board games and card games. We played weekly (as I do now with my new family, Bree). I challenge you to start doing the same.

Good old 'Monopoly' was a family favourite of ours — until my dad and sister Kayla became too serious and it was no longer an enjoyable, playful activity.

I'll confess that I often cheated, as did my mum, while my sister Hannah was always overly concerned about everyone's feelings during the game. She was (and still is) the peacekeeper.

If you see this becoming apparent in your family, change up the game. Make sure it is fun, enjoyable and carefree for everyone. That way you can all get in the flow and reap the benefits of play together.

Playtime for families helps us strengthen our empathy and understanding of one another. It sparks creativity and collaboration. And it supports a level of growth, sturdiness and grit for families as a 'team' — which will come in handy throughout life.

Here are my top tips for helping you make the most of 'playtime' with your family:

» *Experiment with games and playful activities that are enjoyable for everyone.* These games should evoke a carefree atmosphere where everyone can let go, get involved and be on an equal playing field.

» *Set ritualised 'play dates' with your family.* These can be at a certain time each day, or on a certain day of the week. Just make sure everyone is committed because the benefits will be more effective if everyone is present.

» *During every activity, be wholeheartedly present.* Turn off or put away your phone. Turn off the TV. Allow the room to become loud and lit up by the communication between you and your family members.

» *Match your family members' energy levels.* If everyone is loud and boisterous, be like that too. If you feel your family members are wanting to have a relaxing game, allow that to happen without 'forcing' a different atmosphere.

» Let everyone get involved and take the lead at different stages of the game.

» *Stop the game when it is no longer fun, light hearted and enjoyable.* This signals the end of playtime — or you may wish to mix it up, if you feel like the 'play spirit' is still there.

Lack of communication can lead to misunderstandings. Play breaks down these barriers, making tough conversations possible. By incorporating play into their lives, I truly believe families can get through just about anything thrown their way.

Last, but not least

1. Play dates are not only for kids and their friends. We all need play dates in our lives. They can be by yourself, with your partner or with your family and friends. A great way to start is to schedule these in your calendar, diary or weekly agenda. That way they become non-negotiable.

2. Most of us don't allow enough time in our day to slow down and appreciate our own traits and qualities. During 2020 — a year that turned everyone's lives upside down — it was while walking along the beach by myself with no phone that I started to really appreciate myself for who I was. Try reflecting on the person you are by walking with no gadgets, music or distractions. It's truly liberating.

3. The rollercoaster that was 2020 brought with it some wins as well as many losses. Has your health improved in any way due to extra time to exercise, play and be present? Have you started a new hobby or dusted off an old one? Have you found time to appreciate things, places and people you may have taken for granted?

Chapter 10
Play in the classroom

WHAT IS (THANKFULLY) EVIDENT these days is that children don't all learn the same way. As a kid, I needed to move while learning. Sitting, listening and writing were definitely not my fortes. Instead, I found I could remember and become enthusiastic about things if they were taught by way of a game or some form of enjoyable social interaction.

Sitting through university lectures was the same deal. If you'd asked me what I had just listened to for an hour, I wouldn't have been able to tell you anything. But, had you asked me what were the key takeaways from practical sessions and placements in schools (remembering that I was studying to be a teacher!), I could talk about what I had learned for days.

Quite simply, many people retain more information when they learn through play because our brains store this kind of knowledge more deeply.

In classrooms, when play is used to teach, the environment often becomes positive and enthusiastic almost instantly — it's magical. So I always encourage teachers to teach through play if appropriate and possible, and kids to learn through play, particularly if they find sitting still while listening and reading difficult.

I believe that even if a lesson isn't 'textbook' successful, if it is enjoyable and fun, then the takeaways are just as beneficial. 'Play' doesn't always go to plan.

As a teacher, when I was trying to help kids memorise theory related to physical education, I'd often experiment with the best ways of retaining information.

On more than one occasion when doing this, I'd come up with something that was rubbish because I'd been put on the spot. But that never mattered. The playful nature of my method of teaching allowed for mistakes or mishaps. It also empowered the kids to come up with something better than what I had suggested, making it more meaningful and memorable to them. The playful environment inspired them to feel more confident about being creative, problem solving and 'trial-and-error' scenarios.

I believe play assists in unlocking students' full potential, particularly in situations where the learning experience hasn't gone to plan. My vulnerability and admission to what had not played out correctly inspired the students and they felt more equal towards me and safer in the classroom environment.

My 'aha' moment

In 2010 I moved to London on a two-year working visa. I flew to London with a clear image of what it would be like — namely, extremely exciting. It would be an amazing opportunity to earn money, travel around Europe (using London as a base) and grow as a teacher. Little did I know — I was very naïve — how hard teaching in London would be. Man, was it tough!

I lived with my two mates, Azza and Nugget (I know, I know), as well as seven other Aussies in a large, four-bedroom house with one bathroom. With 10 people living in the house, we had a five-minute window each, on a roster, to have a shower and get out of the bathroom so the next person could get ready for work. Sleeping in wasn't an option because a shower on an English winter morning is a must (in the warmer months too because it was always freezing in the mornings compared to what we were used to in Australia).

The three of us had been offered work as casual relief teachers, or 'fill ins'. Each morning, we would get up, have a shower and put on our shirts and slacks. We'd then sit on the couch together in our North Acton townhouse, waiting — just waiting for our teaching agency to ring.

Some days the phone didn't ring at all, but most days an agent would ring and tell us what school we were to attend without offering much information on the context or background of what we'd be walking into. We were kept super busy.

Once we knew which school we were to attend, we'd all spend time figuring out which tube (train) we'd need to catch in order to navigate our way to the school grounds. On arrival, we'd report to the main office. On most occasions, an administration worker would hand us a list of our classes for the day and off we'd go.

Over the six months I did casual relief teaching, the first five were incredibly tough. I had (and still have) never put myself in such a trying and testing situation day in and day out.

On many occasions, I wanted to quit and find a new job, mainly because of the types of schools we were being sent to. They weren't like any other schools I'd taught at before. They were — let me find a nice way of putting it — rough. The cultures of the schools were extremely chaotic. No discipline. No respect for teachers, least of all 'relief' teachers who would fly in for a day possibly never to be seen again. The kids would try to wear you down both mentally and physically. (Yes, I got hit by kids, and hit by things such as cricket bats on more than one occasion.) Now, I'm not saying all the schools I worked at were like this. Some were brilliant, but most were challenging to say the least.

Looking back on the experience now, I don't place blame on the kids at all. I understand why they would try so hard to make my job impossible. I was walking into new classrooms, with new students who had no regard for me, nor did I for them. We had no relationship or bond, so they had no interest in me or the lessons I taught.

Back then, I didn't take the time to make a connection with the students like I did back in Australia — something I prioritise these days.

But then, in the sixth month of my relief teaching stint, I made connecting a priority.

In the sixth month I was sent to a particular central London school for three consecutive days. I was given a heads up beforehand by the teaching agency on how challenging the kids in the class I would be teaching were. It wasn't usual to be warned in this way so I knew almost immediately they had to be beyond tough. Way worse than what I already considered 'the worst'.

The first day I spent with this particular class was hopeless. There was I, with three teaching aides in the class, and not one of the students would sit down. Now, I'm a loud person who has been a PT and fitness instructor for most of my life. Not to mention a team player in multiple sports. But I had never yelled as much as on that first day. To top it off, one of the students had tried to hit me in the back with a cricket bat in the final period when we went outside for some game time. I seriously couldn't think of a more challenging and draining day of my professional career.

I remember feeling so stressed and helpless — clueless as to what to do — that at one stage I sat down at the front of the classroom, put my headphones over my ears and started reading a book.

When the class ended, all I could think about was getting home, calling the teaching agency and telling them I wouldn't (couldn't possibly!) return. How could I face two more days in that hell hole? As much as I felt I needed the money, I just couldn't face it another day.

However, something changed during my tube ride back to North Acton. I had a flashback to my time at high school where I had a relief teacher who started a lesson with four fun, play-based 'connection starter' games (as I now call them). I remembered it as being enjoyable, engaging and a super way for the relief teacher to form a quick bond with us — students he never had taught before and possibly never would again.

In London (much like in Australia) teachers are often left a pile of notes with instructions on what to get through with the class. Surely, I thought, there's no time for games. But somehow, that particular relief teacher at my high school made it work. So why couldn't I?

This moment of reflection was a 'light bulb' moment for me. It was also a memorable moment that shifted how I was, and acted, as a teacher going forward because what I did the next day not only changed my life, but has aided thousands of teachers and students around the world.

On the second day of teaching that 'horrid' class, I walked into the classroom and played four rounds of different games using 'Rock, Paper, Scissors' with the entire class. During these games, there were no winners or losers. It wasn't competitive, but playful and done in jest. The students — who, understandably were resistant at first — soon became amused and engaged in what I was saying and instructing them to do. The day before, I had been yelling and screaming to what seemed like deaf ears. Now, I had these kids listening to me attentively and eating out of my hands. I started to use these glimpses of 'playtime' as an incentive for the kids to behave correctly in class.

For example, I'd say to them, 'After recess and lunch, if you are well behaved, we can play again.' To my surprise, their attitude and willingness to learn changed. They waited anxiously for the next chance to play.

As an aside, I often wonder why we set up classrooms with desks in rows and the teacher at the front. When an artist starts a painting, they have a blank canvas. When a chef wants to create a mouth-watering meal, they start with a clean plate.

The first thing I did (and have always done since) on my second day at this school in London — before playing a connection starter — was to ask the students to move all the chairs and desks to the side of the room. We all paint and cook differently, so why do we think everyone learns the same way? It's insane to keep doing the same thing we have done for years in the classroom. But unfortunately we are creatures of habit.

I found the third day was just as successful as the second — except that it was difficult to continue coming up with different games to keep the kids attentive and entertained. What I found most incredible was that the student who had hit me with the cricket bat two days earlier was now my biggest fan. I had completely turned around the worst day in history to a memorable two days with a group of students who connected and enjoyed each other's qualities.

So, after six gruelling months of relief work, I decided to create a mobile app, which I called ClassBreak. The app houses a suite of engagement starter games that teachers and students can tap into whenever, and wherever, they like. Not only is this app being used by teachers, but also coaches, workplaces and families because the content is designed to suit people of all ages.

What is ClassBreak?

'ClassBreak' is a mobile app designed for teachers all over the world.

The many ideas and games featured in the ClassBreak app will:

» improve your teaching by increasing students' (and adults') engagement and willingness to learn with you

» help instructors, teachers and coaches build confidence in themselves and others, form unity and build self-esteem

» give teachers, specialist teachers and even principals ideas they can use to connect with students on a new level, daily

» help you get to know a new class quickly

» challenge your class with a brainteaser or riddle to get their minds going early in the morning

» help break up lessons using a few quick brain exercises to improve student focus

» provide games and ideas to enhance the last 20 minutes of the school day in a positive way. Starting the day on a high and finishing it with a positive experience are non-negotiables.

Most importantly, ClassBreak can be used anywhere. Just like play. It can be used in the classroom, in the school gym, in a hall, in the workplace or in any outdoor area. Each activity requires minimal (if any) equipment and is extremely easy to explain and set up. It's the perfect pocket app to carry around if you've been given a late replacement class, or if the activity you planned for didn't take up the entire lesson time.

What this situation in London taught me is that it doesn't matter where you are in the world or who you are with, if you don't take the time to connect and build a safe and supportive environment, you're in trouble. No wonder I had an awful time for five months — I was only thinking of myself. When I started sharing myself and listening to the students through play, the barriers came down and the fun started.

What I'm trying to say is that if something isn't working maybe have a look in the mirror because it might be on you. My experience during my first five miserable months in London wasn't the students' fault — it was mine. (**Note to self:** stop being so self-obsessed, Dale!) Share your energy and passion and take time to build relationships everywhere you go in the world.

Last, but not least

1. We are creatures of habit. For as long as classrooms have existed, they have had desks set out in rows or chairs around desks. We assume that everyone learns the same way. Instead, why don't we ask staff and students how they work and learn best and how they would like the room designed? Instead of assuming, let's pass control to the people learning and doing the work.

2. What are your memories of school? Did your learning involve chalk and talk, where the teacher is at the front of the room and the students sit in rows facing the board? If you are still in school, are your classrooms designed to cater for a variety of learning styles?

3. I want to give teachers, students, parents, CEOs and coaches permission to be a maverick and try something new. Just because something isn't broken doesn't mean we can't modify it. The time is right for us to step out of our norm — our comfort zone — and bring some fun and joy back into everything we do. Rant over: I give you permission!

Chapter 11
Team players

BEFORE I START TALKING to the benefits of play for teammates, I want to touch on mateship and its importance in getting you through challenges as a collective. True mateship comes from genuine relationships, which, as we've already established, play helps to foster.

Dr Craig Daly wrote a poem, which you'll find below, that describes true blue mateship. It helped him through a difficult, unforgiving time to see the value in kindness for a team.

Daly's Whinge

It was on a well-worn dirt filled trail, that had played home to countless feet.
Starting down where Davis built his shack.
And ran through jagged hills and fields, where horse and cow would meet.
Some ten miles long when marked both there and back.

It was the kind of trail where stories told were often coloured blue.
The tone of spoken word would make most cringe.
The sternest test to those who laced on boot or shoe.
It became known to all who ran as Daly's Whinge.

The mob who ran were intellects, all employed to mould and teach.
And they did their job with a certain type of flair. But it's hard to make your mark some days when it's hundreds you must reach.
With many of them seeming not to care.

The world of higher education was always heavy in their thoughts,
and they knew they needed plans to get away.
They joined as one in the midday sun, a rehab group of sorts.
With a collective aim to pound their ills away.

There was John the boss with his mop of hair, philosophical with his words.
You'd travel far to meet a man with more finesse.
He was known for loving music, be it Beatles, Stones or Byrds.
A rocker shirt always part of daily dress.

Tony the Brit, with his steely glare, and biceps carved from stone.
With a face that had clearly seen a scrap or two.
Known for standing hard his ground, even outnumbered on his own.
If he said he had your back, you knew it true.

Dashing Don, John's best mate, a nicer bloke you'd never hope to find.
His face set with a permanent toothy smile.
With hands the size of dinner plates, his shake was more a grind.
From a previous life of throwing brick and tile.

The final member of their collective tribe was simply known as Dave.
With a stride that covered ground with panther stealth.
He taught the post grads philosophy, and at home in hidden cave.
Preached to all that environment was wealth.

I joined the group as a tag along for the midday rendezvous.
It's past twenty years but seems like yesterday.
They welcomed me with friendly jest, just like a mate would do.
And called the cattle yards as the track to try that day.

I laughed and said no worries, for I had nothing then to fear.
I knew nothing of the secrets it entailed.
But by the time we'd travelled halfway round I was well back in the rear.
And struggling to grab and use each breath inhaled.

Every hill we met had brothers, each meaner than the first.
And descending down their back a constant grind.
For the track was home to Western Browns, as snakes one of the worst.
Watching where you stepped was front of mind.

And then there came the cattle grates, neglected now for years.
Adorned by spindly grass now overgrown.
A misplaced shoe on one of these would surely end in tears.
For smarter folk this was a no-go zone.

Soon there were the creeks to cross, all up they numbered three.
A branch from side to side the only path.
Where you needed balance of feline, and should your grip come free.
You'd end up soon immersed in a stockman's bath.

At the track's dead end, near a hitching post, it was there that you turned around.
So, the full run had you meet these barriers twice.
And as bad as they were the first time through, heading back with legs unsound.
Wasn't close to anything that you could call nice.

When I discovered this, I took my breath and filled the air with putrid sound.
Using words not found in written prayer.
They let me rattle off my thoughts till I'd soon run out of ground.
And soon laughter filled the hot still country air.

They called me a city whinger, and all four agreed as one.
On a dare for me to match them heading back.
And then they up and disappeared into the shadows of the sun.
So, I started back around that unforgiving track.

By some miracle I summoned strength to get them back in sight.
Although they never seemed to travel all that fast.
The finish line, at Davis shack, was soon there on my right.
And I finished by myself — position last.

My whining went like clockwork. It seemed I rarely missed a day.
When the cattle yards were called as the target quest.
As part of the group's true character, they always let me have my say.
But then they laughed and just ignored my lame request.

With time it lost some venom, the snakes now rare to sight.
The levels in the creeks now safe to vault.
But those hills they still promised misery, and they didn't shirk the fight.
So, I still found time to burden all with fault.

It took near all semester, with attempts now hard to number.
Before my uttered words stopped sounding like a curse.
I knew I had it beaten, when not stopping once for needed rest.
Nor offending those around with working ear.

The group was happy for me, but regardless of that feat.
They agreed that one thing would always stay the same.
And it didn't matter to anyone about the challenge I'd just beat,
Daly's Whinge would always stay its rightful name.

It's taken near on twenty years to understand lessons from their kind.
For I've never claimed to be the smartest in the room.
What I saw as fitness was rather a needed broadening of my mind.
Housework on my attitude with sweeping broom.

Looking back, it was surely needed, an intervention thing of sort.
That delivered at a time when needed most.
For although I didn't show it, the internal battles I had fought.
Had provided me with naught of which to boast.

They gave to me a friendship, and acceptance as a peer.
And more than the many chances that I'd earn.
With my constant groundless whining that would close a clergy's ear.
Any bridge they'd try to build I'd race to burn.

Despite the total of my efforts they'd always hold my place,
never once they left me lonely on the track.
Even when I'd slow to walking, full of harrowed face.
They would call from far ahead then double back.

I guess I'd call it true blue mateship, if pushed to give it name.
And although none of us had been ever called to war,
I imagine it'd be similar if we'd worn the Anzac flame.
For me it ended up as so much more.

'Cause they taught me more than running, or of sticking through dark days.
Or how to cross a creek and stay bone dry.
They showed to me that kindness can come in different ways.
And that it often comes your way for who knows why.

I found that even in life's dust and dirt, there is beauty there to view,
Mostly it's in the journey, not the place you hope to find.
That the core of what one really needs is already inside you.
Often the battle's not with body but with mind.

You see there's always something bubbling that we don't get to understand.
Or others rarely share in honesty about things they fear.
Any little help you give that can free trapped souls from sand,
makes each approaching day a tad more clear.

So, when a Daly's Whinge appears at you, and peace seems out of reach.
Take stock and place your eyes back on the goal.
Think of those intellects on a dusty trail, and the lessons they did teach.
And choose kindness over judgement for your soul.

Now, there's no doubt being a good team member requires us to exert many different skills and qualities. One is kindness, which Craig has touched on. Two others that come to mind are respect and trust.

When we are part of a team, it's paramount that we believe in one another (as well as in ourselves). We need to respect our teammates, not only as sportspeople, but also as individuals with lives away from the sport, perhaps with different beliefs and differing opinions and values.

We are not all the same, which is what makes teams all the more interesting. So, it's extremely important in sport to have respect for the differences among team members.

In a team, you'll be required to form relationships with the various team members. You and your teammates' uniqueness will mean your relationship is unique. Some teammates may be more like you. Some may appear to be starkly different. But the biggest question in all this is, how can we form bonds, no matter who we are? How do we build respect and trust for one another to make us play better and in a more united way?

My answer is simple. We do this through play coupled with an unwavering commitment to our teammates or the sport we're playing.

Organised sport, as we saw in chapter 6 – where I described my experiences with pre-season training schedules – can be incredibly tense and stressful at times. However, these environments afford opportunities to connect and carry the load together.

I find the best way to unite a team and encourage one another to carry the burden is through play-based activities that fall outside the drills and exercises we're used to undertaking together.

Often, you know your team will have your back when it comes to your sport and domain. But will they (and can they) have your back outside of your natural environment together? Most teams are about going into battle, so it's paramount you know you have each other's backs, no matter what.

That's where play makes it interesting. It helps build teams up in a powerful way. Play allows us to test boundaries, get outside of our comfort zones and break down our (and other people's) barriers.

Play permits us to identify what someone is willing to do for us and the team. Particularly when we take 'sport' out of the occasion.

Richard Cheetham told me about one of his research projects when I asked him, 'What is the most intriguing research you've come across when looking at the benefits of adult play?'

His response talks to how coaches of sporting teams perceive play and the importance of having 'playful practitioners' involved to help support teammates and to make individuals feel they are being given permission to play.

Here's what Richard had to say.

The Science of Play

How coaches perceive play

Curiosity got the better of me, so I sought to find out how coaches perceived 'play' and its inclusion in their coaching practice.

Within the research project, I designed a series of activities where they could 'learn to play again' through experiential learning using improvised games and open spaces.

The four key findings were the ease with which they could reconnect with play, to never separate learning from play, to never underestimate the power of play and to create positive play experiences and opportunities for all the age groups they taught. Play was to become integral, never a reward and not just in a warm-up. As one coach reflected, 'I felt we revisited an essential aspect of our growing up ... I wanted to ensure that those feelings and experiences were ones that I could really influence. You only get one chance at childhood!'

Research among adults by Andrew Walsh at the University of Huddersfield in 2019 found that a range of approaches would give them 'permission to play' and a range of circumstances would inhibit it. The perceived 'inappropriateness of play in adult settings' could be countered by providing 'signals' that they could be given permission through 'play enablers'. That once play is forced upon people it is no longer play; that it is voluntary, requires a setting where individuals feel comfortable to play; and that any embarrassment felt would come from being observed by others as 'not playing'. Any approach encouraging adults to play required playful practitioners experienced in enabling it to occur and being mindful of the importance of the 'context in which they are operating'. So, infectious advocates of play are required who can nurture it among other adults, spread the word and create those playful experiences.

It doesn't matter where you are in life, you are part of a number of different teams. You are a team member in so many aspects of your life: with your friends, family, school, work ... Hopefully this chapter has allowed you to see the qualities you have and you bring to each team you are a part of.

Last, but not least

1. The older we get, the smaller our
    friendship groups become. Sad, but true.
    Life becomes busy and we have so much
    going on that we simply don't have the
    time to commit to and nurture all the
    friendships we once had. Not only that, but
    we also don't have the time to deal with people's bullshit,
    so we naturally gravitate to the people who empower and
    complement us.

2. If COVID-19 taught me anything, it's that time is precious
    and so are the connections in my life. I'm guessing you're
    the same and that you now see who your wolf pack is.
    The people who would bend over backwards for you in
    rain, hail or shine. We all have a wolf pack — it just takes
    time for it to mature. Who belongs to your wolf pack?

3. What qualities do you bring to the teams in your life?
    One of the hardest questions I ask people is, 'What are
    your three best qualities?' It's so easy to tell others what
    you love or admire about them, but it makes people
    uncomfortable when the question is thrown back at
    them. I'll take the lead here and tell you my three.
    Try writing down three things you bring to the teams
    you're in.

    Mine are:

    1. I always show up super early with a smile on my face.

    2. I listen and try to be empathetic to everyone I meet
        (this is something that has never come easy, and I
        am still working on making it better).

    3. I am a ball of energy and fun, and will make sure I
        light up any room.

Chapter 12
Play in the workplace and beyond

ALL WORKPLACES ARE INDIVIDUAL, different and unique. But what I have found is that workplaces are similar in the way they often evoke some nervousness and anxiety for newcomers, whether it be on their first day of a new job, or over a longer period of time. When you start a new job, it's not uncommon to be intimidated, in particular when you're trying to understand quickly what the culture is and how everyone behaves.

A playful and fun workplace is often one that makes this transition far easier and more seamless. People feel more comfortable about being themselves sooner. This means less energy is consumed trying to be someone else, giving us more energy for the tasks at hand and for forming deep and meaningful relationships with our colleagues and co-workers.

Play in the workplace has also proven to improve workers' productivity.

Earlier in the book, I mentioned reading an article on the HelpGuide website called 'The benefits of play for adults'.

According to the article, 'playing' at work helps you:

»   remain functional when you are under stress

»   refresh your body and mind

»   work better as a team

»   increase your energy levels, which prevents burnout

»   trigger creativity and innovation

»   observe problems in new ways.

I remember my first day as a teacher (straight out of university) at Orrvale Primary School back in my hometown of Shepparton. For a reason beyond my recollection, right from the beginning of that day I was running 10 minutes behind. Being on time (or early) is something I have always taken pride in, so you can imagine how I felt when I left home late and was rushing. Quite simply, I think I was so nervous that morning, that I had allowed time to get away from me. And those nerves didn't ease, particularly as I entered the staff meeting, which immediately fell to silence.

So here's what I did. When all the conversations stopped, I said as confidently as possible, 'My name is Dale Sidebottom, and I'm late.' I continued (which I probably didn't need to), 'I'm not sure if the road works were as much an issue for you all as they were for me, but *wowee* I've been stuck in them for half an hour!' Now, at this stage everyone in the room had already started laughing. And admittedly, it was pretty funny.

After the laughter died down, the principal (Gail, who was extremely friendly) stood up and said something along the lines of, 'Well, next time you should walk. It'd only take you 20 minutes given you live so close.' Again, everyone laughed unanimously, responding to her playful remark.

I did get a stern warning about being late at the end of the meeting. But the warning ended in laughter because we had already shared a funny encounter.

Workplace culture is determined by the management in charge. At Orrvale Primary School, Gail allowed me to make a blunder on my first day. And instead of hanging me out to dry publicly, she accepted my error rather than turning it into a negative moment for me, which would have ruined my first day.

In doing so, she gained my respect and this made me want to work harder for her, the school and our students. During my year of teaching at Orrvale Primary School, Gail and the rest of the management team were extremely supportive and understanding towards me as a graduate teacher. I will forever be grateful that I had the guidance and love of the team at Orrvale.

Play around the world

As you will have discovered already, I truly believe play is the universal language that connects not only all humans (human to human) but also connects us to animals, and animals to each other (species to species).

When conducted correctly, play accepts everyone. No matter what colour your skin is, how much money you have in your bank account or what sex you are. Play doesn't discriminate. It permits us to be equals, working for the same goal (freedom).

Play has helped me to overcome mental health challenges, which is something I count as a blessing. I will continue to share my story because I don't want to see mental health disrupt and damage communities on a global scale.

In a world often filled with stress, tension and despair, play lets us acknowledge all that is beautiful in life.

We should continue to look at play as something to put on all agendas, in all calendars and at the top of priority lists for adults as well as children all around the world.

Last, but not least

1. Never take yourself too seriously. If you stuff up or do something wrong, own it. If you're late and there is no-one to blame besides yourself, come up with an epic story that is sort of believable. Own it and come in strong. Just make sure it only happens once and you learn from your mistake. This applies to life and work. A mistake is a mistake once; when it happens more than once, it's an issue.

2. Work and life should never be completely serious. If you are not smiling at work or in life, then you need to stop right now and change! Change your job, your outlook on life or the people you are hanging around with. Life is meant to be fun, beautiful and playful. If it's not, it's on you to sort this out ASAP.

3. We all need more Gails in our lives. I've had some great bosses over the years, and some not so great bosses. Think back to who was in charge when you stuffed up? The stuff-up can be small, medium or large. Did this leader make you feel as good as Gail made me feel on my first day in the full-time workforce? If so, that's brilliant. If not, that's also fine. When you are the boss, in charge or the leader of a team, remember this: don't make the same mistakes that were made on you! #bemoregail

part IV

PLAY *in* ACTION

Chapter 13
The play-based mindfulness toolkit

IN CHAPTERS 14, 15 AND 16, I'm going to show you some 'tools' for injecting more play and mindfulness into each and every day. These are a selection of the games and activities that you'll find on my websites, Jugar Life, Energetic Education and Fitness Games Zone.

While these tools are explained here, I have also added QR codes that will take you to additional resources so you can see these games and activities in action.

As you'll discover, almost all of these tools revolve around 'The Daily PEGG' ritual, which I touched on in chapter 4. While the idea is to use these tools as part of The Daily PEGG, these games and activities can be played anywhere, anytime.

The Daily PEGG

The Daily PEGG is a ritual that was born in 2019 and has since been practised by thousands of students, teachers, teams, families and corporates on a daily basis. The 'PEGG' in 'Daily PEGG' stands for 'play, exercise, gratitude and giving'.

Since creating The Daily PEGG and including it in my life, I have found that on the days when I don't use it — or don't consciously practise play, exercise, gratitude and giving — I'm not my cheerful energetic self.

So I encourage you to give it a try. Here's how you do it.

The Daily PEGG is simple. You need to focus on including all four puzzle pieces (play, exercise, gratitude and giving) in your day:

» *Play* is anything that gets you in the 'flow'. It's whatever makes you feel completely present, unrestricted, engaged and elated. It can be simple things like knitting, playing a game of cards with a friend, colouring in or skipping like a child on a pavement. Whatever it is, make sure play becomes part of your everyday.

» *Exercise* is any activity that gets your body moving, whether it's going for a walk, a jog, a ride or a swim, or perhaps dancing.

» *Gratitude* is about finding time in your day to step back and be thankful for your life, the world around you and the awesome people in your life. It's practising appreciation.

» *Giving* is carrying out an act of kindness for somebody else without the expectation of receiving something in return. Giving requires you to think about someone else's happiness — what would lift their mood or their day — and making sure you take action as part of the four core steps.

Now, the idea is that once you've completed these four core activities (bear with me — I know it's ridiculous, but that's the point!) you need to get a peg and clip it somewhere on your body, be it on your nose, on an ear, in your hair — wherever you like!

And that's The Daily PEGG. It's childish in spirit. It's simple. And it's ultra-effective for making every day the best it can be. I encourage you to introduce The Daily PEGG into your work culture and personal life — and make it a non-negotiable.

Daily mission cards

To complement The Daily PEGG I developed a unique set of cards I call 'daily mission cards'. They're playful in nature and will instruct and empower you to take on one 'playful' mission each day. There are heaps of cards to choose from so you'll never run out of daily play, exercise, gratitude or giving ideas.

Rather than explain these cards, I'll let the cards do the talking. Here are a few of my favourite daily mission cards (some of which I developed with Richard Cheetham).

Using the 12 cards shown here, select seven different cards and try to act on one each day for the next week.

Backwards Winner

Today, your challenge when walking through any door is to do so walking backwards.

Smile Smile Smile

Your mission today is to smile and laugh throughout the day. This might mean telling a funny joke or watching a comedy show. Your task is to try and make people smile with you.

Sneaky Sneaky

Today, your mission is to try and hide like a ninja and scare as many people as possible. The more people you scare, the better.

Straight Face

Today, your mission is to play the straight face game with three different people. Take it in turns to try and make the other person laugh for 10 seconds. The aim is to keep a straight face. First person to laugh or smile loses.

Knee Tag

Play a game of knee tag with three different people today. To play, face your partner and try and tag their knee with your hands before they can tag your knees. First, to tag five times wins.

Push-ups

Today, anytime you see a bench or raised item, try to complete five push-ups on it. See how many you can do for the entire day.

Shake & Bake

Today, your mission is to create three unique handshakes with three different people. Each time you see them, you will perform your new handshake together.

Shoulder Tag

Play a game of shoulder tag with three different people today. To play, you face your partner and use your hands to try and tag either of your partner's shoulders before they can tag yours. First to five tags wins.

Playground Fun

Today, your mission is to visit a playground. What are the various activities you can do on the playground? How many ways can you move your body on the playground equipment?

Recharge

Your mission today is to try to introduce 30 minutes of solitude, no talking just sitting with your thoughts outdoors. Try to rest and recharge both your body and your mind.

Toilet Paper

Today, we would like you to use a toilet paper roll. What can you do with a roll of toilet paper? How creative can you be?

Missing Chair

Is it possible to stand all day? Can you go the entire day without using a seat or chair? You can kneel or sit on the floor if needed.

Chapter 14

PEGG: Play options

THE FOLLOWING FOUR GAMES are what I call 'connection starters'. I have already mentioned how I use these in everything I do. They are easy to play and understand, and the best thing is they are suited for people of all ages. Not only that, they will put a smile on everyone's dial as well. Just like Colonel Sanders with his 11 secret herbs and spices, these are my secret games to build fun, trust and connection wherever you are.

'One, Two, Three'

This game was inspired by Ryan Ellis, founder of and teacher at The PE Umbrella. There are two versions of 'One, Two, Three': a standard game and a fitness version. The first is a simple version with actions. The second has been modified to include a fitness aspect so you're playing but also really getting your body moving.

Standard game

Players: 2 or more (even numbers as you'll need to pair off)

Aim of the game: laughter

Instructions:

Level 1: Partner with someone, standing face to face one metre apart. Begin counting from 1 to 3 in turns (so, if I was going first, I would say '1', before you say '2'. Then I would say '3' before you say '1', then I say '2', and so on). The faster you can do this, the better.

Level 2: Now things get interesting. You need to start adding movement to the numbers. Start by adding a clap instead of saying the number '1' as you continue to take it in turns. So, instead of saying '1', you clap once. At this level, the numbers 2 and 3 remain without actions, the same as for the first level.

Level 3: Next we add a simple action instead of saying the number 2. Every time you or your partner is meant to say '2', you must bow. The number 1 stays the same (a clap) and the number 3 stays the same (you say the number 3). You will hear a clap, then see a bow and then hear the number 3. Again, the faster you can go, the better.

Level 4: It's time to add in the final action, which is to put your hands in the air instead of saying the number 3. This means in this final round you will not hear any numbers at all. Just actions — and laughter, of course. So, every time it's your turn to say '3', throw your hands in the air. During this final round it's all action — 1 is the clap, 2 is the bow and 3 is hands straight up in the air.

Fitness version

Players: 2 or more (even numbers as you'll need to pair off)

Aim of the game: laughter and getting the body bumping!

Instructions:

Level 1: Partner with someone, standing face to face one metre apart. Begin counting from 1 to 3 in turns (so, if I was going first, I would say '1', before you say '2'. Then I would say '3' before you say '1', then I would say '2', and so on). The faster you can do this, the better.

Level 2: Now things get interesting. You need to start adding a fitness move to the numbers. Start by adding a squat instead of saying the number '1' as you continue to take it in turns. So, instead of saying '1', you squat once. At this level, the numbers 2 and 3 remain without any fitness move, the same as for the first level.

Level 3: Next it's time to add a fitness move instead of saying the number 2. Every time you or your partner is meant to say '2', you must do a star jump. So, one of you begins by doing a squat instead of saying '1' and the other does a star jump instead of saying '2'. The number '3' stays the same. Again, the faster you can go, the better.

Level 4: It's time to add in the final fitness move, which is to do a burpee whenever it's your turn to say the number 3. This means in this final round you will not hear any numbers at all. Just actions — and laughter, of course.

Ready to play? Check out this tutorial video.[5] (It's much easier to understand if you watch the play-based game in action!)

[5] **Follow the QR code to see how to play 'One, Two, Three'.**

'Three Is a Charm'

This is a game you can play remotely, face to face or digitally with others. It's a great 'icebreaker' and one I used with former professional surfer and seven-time world champion, Layne Beachley, when I invited her onto my podcast. Similarly to the previous game, I'll provide you with two versions of this game.

Standard game

Players: 2 or more (even numbers as you'll need to pair off)

Aim of the game: laughter, connection and team building

Instructions:

Partner up with somebody and take it in turns to count as high as you can together. But on all 'multiples' of 3 (6, 9, 12, 15, 18 and so on) you need to say your partner's name instead of the number. Also, for any number that has a 3 in it you need to say your partner's name instead of the number. These numbers are 13 and 23. If you get to 30 without making a mistake, you win the game.

There are modified versions of this game below to challenge you when you are able to get to 30 in this version.

The aim of the game is to see how high you can get before somebody mucks up. When that happens, you need to go back to 1 and start again.

Modified game

Players: 2 or more (even numbers as you'll need to pair up)

Aim of the game: laughter, connection, team building and movement

Instructions:

Modification 1: Follow the instructions for the standard game but hold a squat until you reach a multiple of 3 and say your partner's name. As soon as you say their name, you have to lift out of the squat and then go back into the squat.

Modification 2: Follow the above instructions but instead of saying your partner's name every time you land on a multiple of 3, shout out the name of a capital city (or pick a topic you love and create your own themed idea). You can try this version of the game either by adding the movement exercise (such as the squat, as above) or without the physical element.

This video[6] will explain it further for you.

I love using this game in keynotes and workshops. I design the topic to suit the industry or audience. Instead of saying a capital city on multiples of 3 I would pick a theme. For example, when I was working with L'Oréal the theme was products that L'Oréal sold; and with Cricket Australia executives I used players' names or rules of the game. You can design it to suit your audience. It's such a great way to build connections around the theme or industry you are working with or in.

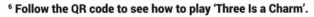

[6] **Follow the QR code to see how to play 'Three Is a Charm'.**

'Clapping: 1, 2, 3'

This game is suited for large groups.

Players: 8 or more (I have played this with upwards of 100 people)

Aim of the game: laughter, connection and team building

Instructions:

All participants (8 or more) stand in a circle (or the 'rhythm master' — who forms a beat by clapping, tapping their knees and clapping again — can be at the front of the room and everyone faces them). Everyone else has to try their best to keep the beat with the 'rhythm master' as the number of movements increase.

Role of the rhythm master:

1. Start off with a simple beat by clapping *once*, tapping your knees and then clapping *once* again.

2. Instruct people that when you say '2' they are to clap twice, tap their knees twice and then clap twice again.

3. Instruct them that when you say '3' they are to clap three times, tap their knees three times (in a row) and then clap three times again.

This will require practice by you and the group. But eventually, you'll be able to mix it up by calling out different number sequences; for example, '2, 1'; '3, 2'; '1, 2, 3'.

If you watched my TEDx Talk, you would have seen this game in action. To watch it again, here is the video.[7]

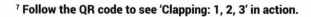

[7] Follow the QR code to see 'Clapping: 1, 2, 3' in action.

'Drawing Animals on Your Head'

Players: 2 or more (as a group or in pairs)

Aim of the game: laughter, guessing, creativity and curiosity

Materials required: a pen, pencil or Texta; a piece of paper. It's also helpful to have a solid backing to place your paper on (such as a clipboard). Without it, drawing on your head can be difficult!

Instructions:

Step 1: Give every participant around 30 seconds to draw something from a specific category (without revealing what it is). The category I usually use is 'animals', but this isn't mandatory. You can choose whatever category you like.

Now this might sound easy, but the trick is to get everyone to draw their selected animal/object using their head as a table/base (this is where the clipboard comes in handy).

That way, the shapes become warped and hard to identify.

Step 2: Once the 30 seconds is up, everyone takes it in turns to reveal their animal/object after the rest of the group (or your partner) has played a guessing game around what it is!

This video[8] will help explain the game further.

---

[8] Follow the QR code to see how to play 'Drawing Animals on Your Head'.

Chapter 15
PEGG: Exercise options

SOMETIMES IT CAN BE a challenge to make fitness-based activities enjoyable. That's why these three examples are grounded in play but still overarchingly involve movement and exercise.

'Spring Racing Carnival'

This game was inspired by the horse racing in Melbourne.

Players: 2 or more

Aim of the game: body movement, laughter, enjoyment (to win is always nice!)

Materials required: 1 six-sided die; 10 pieces of paper and a pen, pencil or Texta: our Fun Fitness daily mission cards (optional)

Instructions:

Step 1: You play this game as an individual (against other 'competitors').

Start off by picking a funny horse name. Some of my all-time favourites are Hoof Hearted, Wearthefoxhat, Maythehorsebwithu, Red Hot Filly Pepper and Passing Wind.

Step 2: Once you've picked your name as a group (or pair), choose 10 different fitness exercises. Write each one down on a separate piece of paper. Alternatively, you can use the Fun Fitness daily mission cards. For the purpose of this exercise, I'll explain it as though you don't have these on hand.

These exercises could include star jumps, push-ups, squats, burpees, sit-ups, leg raises, lunges and squat jumps (any movements you like).

Step 3: Once you have written these down, place each exercise in front of your group (or pair) — approximately 10 metres apart — in a straight line. Each of these pieces of paper with exercises written on them (or Fun Fitness mission cards) will become individual stations.

Step 4: The game starts at a 'starting line', which is the first station.

Step 5: You each then – in turn – roll the die to dictate your next move.

Rolled a 1? Move back one spot (so, back to the starting line or back to the station prior to the one you are at). Either way, do 10 repetitions of the exercise written on the station you land on.

Rolled a 2 or a 3? Stay where you are and complete 10 repetitions of the exercise on that station.

Rolled a 4 or a 5? Move to the next station and do 10 repetitions of the exercise at that station.

Rolled a 6? Move ahead two stations and do 10 repetitions of the exercise at that station.

Step 6: The aim is to reach the finish line first. It's up to luck (not your fitness level), which makes it an enjoyable, even playing field!

Giddy up!

Watch this video[9] for a more detailed explanation of the game.

---

[9] **Follow the QR code to see how to play 'Spring Racing Carnival'.**

'UNO Fitness'

There are two versions of this play-based exercise game.

Standard version

Players: 1 or more

Aim of the game: body movement, laughter, enjoyment

Materials required: one pack of UNO cards (108 cards); a timer

Instructions:

For this game, you need to set a timer for 10 minutes. Use a set of UNO cards to dictate what actions or exercises you do next. See the list of what card relates to what action below. Use the numbers of the cards to dictate how many reps you do. For example, selecting a yellow 5 means you need to complete five push-ups before selecting a new card.

YELLOW: Push-ups

GREEN: Sit-ups

BLUE: Squats

RED: Squat thrusters

SKIP: Double of the next card

REVERSE: Complete the previous card again

DRAW 2: Complete 20 reps of the next coloured card

DRAW 4: 1 × 30-second plank hold

WILD: 4 burpees

Note: If you don't have a set of UNO cards, you could use a deck of normal playing cards and use the different suits for the colours, and the picture cards can be the other cards. As with the UNO game, if the heart cards were push-ups, and you selected a 5 of hearts you would need to complete five push-ups before selecting another card.

Harder version

Players: 1 or more

Aim of the game: body movement, laughter, enjoyment

Materials required: one pack of UNO cards (108 cards); a timer

Instructions:

For this game, the aim is to make your way through an entire pack of UNO cards (108). Use the cards to dictate your exercises. See the list of what card relates to what action below. And remember — the number on the card will tell you how many reps to do!

I like to set a timer for this option, and record how long it takes to finish all 108 cards. Record this time and then the next time you play, you have a score to beat.

YELLOW: Push-ups

GREEN: Sit-ups

BLUE: Squats

RED: Squat thrusters

SKIP: Double of the next card

REVERSE: Complete the previous card again

DRAW 2: Complete 20 reps of the next coloured card

DRAW 4: 1 × 30-second plank hold

WILD: 4 burpees

Watch this video[10] for a tutorial on this body-moving game of UNO!

---

[10] **Follow the QR code to see how to play 'UNO Fitness'.**

'Build 'Em Up Cards'

Players: 1 or more

Aim of the game: body movement, laughter, enjoyment

Materials required: one standard deck of cards (52 cards), a timer

Instructions:

The aim of this game is to finish a 15-minute exercise session with as many cards as possible in front of you — or at least more than there are in front of your opponent/s.

Start by shuffling the deck and placing it face down in front of you. Start the timer at 15 minutes. Each person selects a card, lays it in front of them face up and completes the exercise that relates to it from the list below as quickly as they can.

2: 10 × mountain climbers

3: 10 × beetle jumps

4: 10 × alternate lunge jumps

5: 10 × dips

6: 10 × Russian twists

7: 10 × leg raises

8: 10 × donkey kicks

9: 10 × commandos

10: 10 × plank jacks

Jack: 10 × pistol squats (5 on each leg)

Queen: 10 × push-ups

King: 10 × sumo jump squats

Ace: 10 × squat thrusters

Joker: 5 × burpees and a 200-metre run!

Everyone then picks up another card, lays it next to the first one and completes that exercise *and* the one on their previous card before picking up a third card ... and so on. Each time a player picks up a new card from the deck, they have to complete the related exercise as well as all the previous ones — in other words, they build 'em up! The more cards you get, the longer it takes to complete all your exercises.

The winner is the person who has the most cards in front of them after 15 minutes.

There's one more thing: if you pick up the Joker you have to call out 'Joker!' and everyone *except you* has to stop what they are doing and do 5 burpees and a 200-metre run (you'll need to determine where to run to before starting the game). You can pick up another card and continue with your exercises and everyone else has to take up from where they left off after they have done the Joker exercise.

Watch this video[11] for a visual explanation of the game.

If you're not familiar with how to do all of the exercises above, check out this video[12] to see the best 30 body weight fitness exercises ever created in action!

---

[11] **Follow the QR code to see how to play 'Build 'Em Up Cards'.**

[12] **Follow the QR code to see the best 30 body weight fitness exercises.**

Chapter 16
PEGG: Gratitude and Giving options

BEING KIND AND DOING nice things can sometimes be too open-ended and hard to figure out. Let me show you what true giving can look like in a fun and caring way. And how gratitude can be sexy and engaging. Dive into these two powerful Gs to finish off your Daily PEGG.

G — *Gratitude options*

Three Gratitude cards

Do you want to start your meeting with a bang? Kick that social dinner off with a thought-provoking question? Commence the day or week with gratitude? Or maybe generate some quality questions as a family around the dinner table each night?

I designed my three daily mission 'Gratitude' cards for that very purpose. The first card contains a selection of 'morning starter' gratitude questions. The second one has questions you can use throughout the day. And the third card lists some 'evening reflection' gratitude questions.

Instead of describing the Gratitude cards to you, let me show them to you. You can ask people to select a number between 1 and 6 (there are six questions on each card) or if you have a six-sided die, have some fun rolling the die to see what gratitude questions you will share or reflect on.

Morning starter

1. What am I looking forward to today?

2. Who am I excited to see today and why?

3. What am I going to do really well today?

4. When I woke up this morning, I was very grateful for...

5. What is something I can do to make someone else's day better?

6. What is something that is going to make me feel happy today?

Gratitude discussion

1. What is something I can see at this moment that makes me happy?

2. What's the best thing I have done in the last week?

3. Today I am excited to see... Because....

4. I get excited when I....

5. If I had one wish today, I would wish for...

6. Today I am very proud of....

Evening reflection

1. What was something I did well today?

2. What was the biggest win I had today?

3. What did I learn today about myself and others?

4. What are two things I am grateful for after today?

5. What are you most looking forward to about tomorrow?

6. How did I make someone's day better with an action or gesture?

The Gratitude Wall

One simple activity you can do at home, at school or in the workplace is create a 'gratitude wall'. Ask the questions on my three daily mission Gratitude cards and write your answers on sticky notes. Then stick them in a place you frequent, forming a 'gratitude wall'. You can do this on your own or with a group of people. It can be a powerful reminder of all the amazing things you are appreciative of and thankful for.

Happiness inspires more happiness, so the more you can get involved in this activity, the better. It also makes for some quality artwork, which will seriously inspire more gratitude when people see your wall.

G — Giving options

The 'Giving' daily mission cards

As you will by now have discovered, I use daily mission cards quite a lot. Whether through play, for fitness activities or for gratitude and giving.

My Giving daily mission cards have been created to make it easier for you to come up with simple ways you can make giving part of every day.

Use these cards however you like — whether it's one a day, or all nine daily! I challenge you to complete one of these cards each day over a nine-day period. I bet it will make you feel unbelievably good!

Leave a positive sticky note on someone's desk or in their office.

Random act of kindness, paying it forward. Buy someone's coffee, petrol or a meal.

Find opportunities to give five compliments. It costs nothing, takes no time and could make someone's entire day. Don't just think about it. Say it.

Do a chore, task or job today for someone without them knowing.

Ask a friend to complete an empathy walk with you today. Where you take it in turns to talk and walk. One is talking, the other is listening. You get five minutes each to talk about anything you like.

Be kind to yourself today. Write down three to five things for which you're grateful. Do this at the end of the day in the Jugar Life app, your journal or as a picture for yourself.

Today your challenge is to make the world a cleaner place. Pick up any litter or rubbish that you see laying around.

Say 'thank you' to someone who made a difference ... Please explain this to them either verbally or in written form.

Do a favour today for someone, without asking for anything in return.

The 'Giving' scale

Andy Milne is a health and physical education teacher based in the United States. He is the creator of the 'giving' scale (below) and the hugely popular 'Slow Chat Health' blog and website. Andy is a great friend and an inspiration to teachers all around the world.

This is a simple activity. All you need to do is reach out to someone and ask them how they are feeling out of 10. 1 = extremely unhappy. 10 = elated.

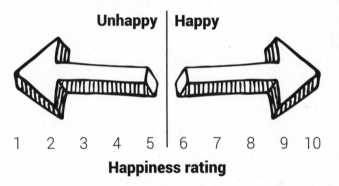

Unhappy | **Happy**

1   2   3   4   5   6   7   8   9   10

Happiness rating

When they provide you with a number, you should ask them, 'How can I make that number higher for you?'

For example, someone may say, '5 — because I'm feeling flat and stressed and don't have time to do my house chores.' You can then offer to provide support and possibly help that person move to a 7 or an 8.

I use this activity a lot with my family members and my wife Bree. It's a great way to open up conversations and generate meaningful 'giving'.

It might sound silly, but the simplicity of this act of kindness is why it is so powerful. Give it a try with someone in your life today.

PAL message (kindness boomerang)

If you are up for a giving challenge, try this: '100 days of letting people in your life know what they mean to you'.

PAL stands for 'proud, admire and love' and there is more on this in part V where I talk about ritualising play-based mindfulness.

PAL works like this: choose a (different) person every day for 100 days and let them know why you are proud of them, why you admire them and why you love (or respect) them.

I set myself this 100-day challenge and it helped me to reconnect with friends, family and others I had lost contact with or severed relationships with when I was at my worst. You don't have to start with 100 days — maybe try 10 and see the impact it has. I originally thought I would try this with 10 people and then after seeing how successful it was I knew I had to make it much bigger, which is why I did it for 100 days straight.

Each morning, I would set myself a challenge to reach out to one person with a message that began something like this:

Dear X, please don't feel as though you have to reply to me, but there are a few things I wanted to say to you.

I would then take the time to write a paragraph about why I was proud of them, what I admired about them and what I loved about them or why I loved them.

This was unnatural for me — and incredibly scary. I felt very vulnerable. But I eventually got over this because I saw the benefits of putting these beautiful messages out into the world.

You always need to prepare yourself for mixed responses. I had grown men, who had never shared emotions with me, ring me crying. I had people call me to see if I was okay! It just shows how irregular these messages are in people's lives, making them so wonderful and distinctive.

As you start putting meaningful messages out into the world, eventually you'll start to receive them too. And your relationships with others will improve tenfold. Which is why I often refer to the PAL message as a 'kindness boomerang'.

PAL not only provides others with glimpses of happiness in their day, but also gives you a sense of fulfilment.

part V

NEVER *stop* PLAYING

Chapter 17
Being mindful

LET'S BE HONEST, FINDING a meaning for the term 'mindfulness' can be pretty confusing. The key to ritualising play-based mindfulness in your daily calendar is trial and error. Everyone is different and one size shoe doesn't fit all. Finding a routine that suits your personality, schedule and needs is personal.

The key is not to give up. Like learning a new language, riding a bike or learning a new skill, it takes time, practice and an open mind. It has taken me 30-odd years to find a routine that works for me, and even now it's still changing as my life changes. In this chapter, I will do my best to share what has worked for me and lots of people around the world with whom I have shared my story, passion and knowledge.

The play and mindfulness trap

Busy is not a badge of honour. So, if you're ready, I say it's time to slow down the hamster wheel (or treadmill!). Start taking more time for yourself and rediscovering (or reprioritising) what's important in your life and deserves the most attention.

You'll be able to do this if you allow yourself to stop, breathe and focus on what's in the present. Stopping and giving yourself time and space is also a pathway towards practising mindfulness.

For years, as you've learned, I saw the word 'busy' as something to be extremely proud of. I'm still not sure why! But I can assure you that 'busy' won't bring about happiness. It's more likely to lead to you and those around you — the ones you're 'too busy' to spend time with — being disappointed .

Busy schedules are part of the world we live in. And we all know there are a lot of busy people out there. People who long to take time out during their day to reconnect with their reality and find time for mindfulness. That's the mindfulness trap! We need to find time to be present and aware of our surroundings — to stop just being human for a while.

However, mindfulness is often hard to prioritise so it can quickly become the least important part of a very long list of tasks. To ensure mindfulness becomes not only a priority, but also a ritual and somewhat of a habit, we need to make it quick and easy to accomplish — often. And it helps to make everything we do fun because when activities, tasks or chores are fun we are much more inclined to stick to them.

So don't let yourself fall into the mindfulness trap. To avoid ditching the routine of mindfulness early, my belief is that you should set yourself up for a 'win' every day. I like to start my day by practising mindfulness first thing in the morning because I know this works. It sets my day up for success. It's these early wins that I believe are the key to success, so I encourage you to inject mindfulness into your morning routine.

Now, what do I mean when I say 'early wins' are the key to success? Well, a lot of the time we are bombarded with deadlines, meetings and appointments. Our days become filled with other people who have a say in and potential control over our actions, thoughts and attention. So it's important to take moments for yourself as early in the day as you can.

Taking control of my mornings was a significant game changer for me. I used to allow my mornings to start in a spin. My mind was constantly on work and the tasks that needed to be done. So even as I woke, I was already in a fluster about the day ahead and everything requiring my attention. My adrenaline was pumping and it wouldn't stop until I passed out with exhaustion at the end of the day.

For me, even the most mundane and simple tasks have become part of my 'early wins'. For example, every day I get up early, and the first thing I do is make my bed. This is a small win. It allows me to feel I have achieved something before I even step outside my bedroom.

For me, practising mindfulness in the morning is a key win. It decreases the grey matter in the learning parts of the brain. Practising mindfulness first thing in the morning has the proven benefits of decreasing stress early on and balancing the activity level of thoughts in your prefrontal cortex, which is responsible for your emotions, your problem-solving skills and your ability to plan for and around things.

Of course, our lives are such that not everyone will be able to have exactly the same morning routine. So, it's important you focus on what feels right, simple and achievable for you. But what we can collectively get good at is looking at every day as though it's a match (one big game). Without pre-season, how can we possibly get through the day's challenges?

Ritualising play-based mindfulness

I'd like to share a 20-minute morning routine that you can emulate if it works for you. This routine has allowed me to ritualise mindfulness and not fall into the mindfulness trap by letting mindfulness fall down the ladder of priorities.

You can watch a video of my routine[13], or I've captured the key steps below.

Note: there's an instruction to download my free 'Jugar Life' app. Jugar Life is the umbrella word I use to talk about everything I stand for in life: play-based mindfulness, gratitude and fitness. *Jugar* in Spanish means 'to play'. Jugar Life aims to give you all the tools you need to take control of your life and find glimpses of happiness each and every day.

The app contains an 'AM' section and a 'PM' section, which I'll take you through now.

Play-based mindfulness: morning routine

The night before:

1. *Prepare to start your day earlier:* Make a conscious decision to start your day earlier than planned. Set your alarm half an hour earlier than you normally would.

----

[13] **Follow this QR code to see my routine.**

2. *Download my Jugar Life app:* This is so you can be led through my 20-minute morning routine until it's part of your everyday.

3. *Turn off your phone notifications:* To set yourself up for a mindful morning, I recommend ensuring your phone is on flight mode before you fall asleep.

   All my workaholic life, this is something I never did. As a result, my brain was disrupted by notifications and noises when I was sleeping. It also meant that my brain was focused solely on my emails and messages as soon as I woke up to start my day. To avoid this, turn off notifications and place your phone away so you can't see it.

In the morning:

1. *Make your bed:* When your alarm goes off, get straight out of bed and make your bed! This is one of the 'little wins' I spoke about earlier that will help you build good, structured habits.

2. *Drink water:* The next step is to drink half a litre of water. Water hydrates you, flushes out toxins and sets your brain up for a healthy day.

3. *Open the Jugar Life app:* You'll automatically be taken to 'Day 1' and be prompted to answer the three morning routine questions: 'What are you excited about today?', 'What might challenge you today?' and 'How can I surprise somebody today with an act of kindness?'

   The first question — 'What are you excited about today?' — will start your brain off thinking positively. You'll begin the day by identifying what you have coming up that you are, or should be, looking forward to.

The second question — 'What might challenge you today?' — will help you identify and eliminate challenging situations early.

The third question — 'How can I surprise somebody today with an act of kindness?' is where PAL comes in, or is when to give a Daily Mission Card a go.

We looked at the PAL framework in part IV, but here's a recap. PAL stands for 'proud, admire and love'. The idea is to identify a loved one, friend or colleague and send them an unexpected message about why you are proud of them, admire them and love (or respect) them. This will make them feel better and in turn, will make you happy too. And it will have a significant effect on the rest of your day. This will release the love drug oxytocin and kick-start your day the right way.

4. *Move your body:* The next step is to spend 10 minutes getting your body moving and your blood flowing with some form of exercise that you enjoy. This could be a walk, a quick swim, a ride, or a simple exercise inside your house. This step is crucial because it will increase your energy levels and release endorphins, which help to create a positive mindset, keeping your mind sharp and enthusiastic throughout the day.

5. *Practise presence and calm:* Re-open the Jugar Life app and select just one of the 15 breathing routines. Find a quiet, comfortable position where you won't be interrupted or distracted and complete your chosen task for two to three minutes.

By practising this 20-minute morning routine, you're spending a small amount of time and achieving a whole lot. You have set your morning up with the Jugar Life morning questions. You have made somebody else's day better with the PAL kindness message. You have got your body moving and your blood flowing with your 10 minutes of exercise. And you have become calm and present with your breathing and meditation.

It's now time to switch off 'flight mode' and tackle the day! Put your seat belt on and block out the turbulence of life.

Play-based mindfulness: evening routine

Once you're in the swing of practising play-based mindfulness every morning, I challenge you to start introducing the Jugar Life journalling questions at the end of your day. It's important to note — as we all know that screen time can make it more challenging to wind down and sleep — that once you have completed your Jugar Life questions, you should set your alarm, put your phone on flight mode and then not touch it again until morning!

The evening journalling questions are:

1. What are three things I am grateful for or the biggest wins I had for the day?

2. What form of play did I do today and how did it make me feel?

3. What did I learn today?

As you can see, the first question prompts you to focus solely on the positives that came about during the day as well as any big or little 'wins'.

The second question helps you get into the routine of being accountable for your short bursts of play throughout the day and focus on the feelings these play-based activities brought about.

The final question is set up to encourage you to see the day as something you've learned from. Embracing the notion that you'll continue to grow and develop is a great way to send yourself off to sleep, ready for the next morning routine ahead!

The key to being mindful and allowing yourself to find forms of play-based mindfulness for yourself and others is starting and finishing your day with a positive. Like most things in life that are good for us, we need to allow time in our day for mindfulness, otherwise we will very quickly slip back into our old ways and the mindfulness trap will put us back on the hamster wheel of life.

Don't beat yourself up though if you do slip back. We are all human and we fall off the wagon. I am far from perfect, and there are days where things get completely derailed. The key is to go to bed and start the next day the right way. Win the day, win the week ... and so on. It's a process that is worth the hard work and dedication — you can trust me on that!

TEN FINAL LESSONS

WRITING THIS BOOK HAS been incredibly soothing for me. It has made me think more and more about what's important in life. After a few Zoom calls with Dr Craig Daly, who has featured a lot in the book, I put together 10 'lessons' that I think will act as a good takeout.

I hope my future children will read these to learn more about me and especially to learn from my life's mistakes and the experiences I endured for more than 30 years.

What I've learned through my many ups and downs is that life is unpredictable. It provides experiences that can manifest in both happiness and regret. Hopefully my story, and my lessons, help to put you on a path to happiness (and not regret).

Here are the 10 lessons I'd like to leave you with that I hope will bring you sustained happiness.

Lesson 1: Don't let education get in the way of your learning

In high school, my English teacher implored us to not let education get in the way of our learning. She argued that there was more to the world than what's offered through formal education, and that real learning takes place outside the walls of any institution.

It felt like poor timing when she said this just as we were about to graduate (that is, after we had endured gruelling years of textbooks and exams)! But she was absolutely correct. Thank you, Ms Sleeth.

Don't let the education you receive at school or university become the only form of learning you seek and prioritise in life. I don't mean don't take education seriously. But always prepare to keep learning. Stay curious and commit to developing day by day. And passionately pursue anything that gives you knowledge. Because knowledge provides both understanding and opportunity.

Most importantly, be ready to 'unlearn' as well. Some of the things you learn, and habits you grow into, may be damaging, tainted and downright wrong. You may learn to prioritise things that are at odds with having a harmonious life. So, be prepared to put your thoughts, words and actions under a microscope as you age. Be ready to 'unlearn' and be ready to take action.

Lesson 2: Invest in people

As many of us start work and receive a comfortable income, we often look at starting our investment journey. It's here that many of us fail to acknowledge the world's greatest assets, which we've been investing in for years: people.

No — your greatest assets in life will not be managed funds, real estate or bitcoin. Relationships will be the highest paying and most fulfilling investment you make in life.

Investing in relationships is no different from any other investment. It takes understanding, commitment, courage and patience to experience tangible growth.

Yes, there will be times when you will occasionally be or feel burned. Relationships may make you feel disappointed, angry or hurt. But good investments (relationships) won't make you feel this way forever. Every day we stay invested in relationships provides another opportunity for professional and personal return. You just need to handle the bumps along the way. Stay in it for the long haul and witness the growth, which is overwhelmingly rewarding.

Lesson 3: Keep serving

Be kind to others, and serve them with simple acts of kindness — it's one of the most simple and gratifying pleasures in life. But these acts of kindness need to be done out of sincerity, without the expectation of receiving something in return.

As you grow, don't be a score keeper. Forget about being paid back, and always pay forward.

Serving others can help develop a sense of purpose and meaning in life. Do it because it's the right thing to do. We need more kindness in our world.

Lesson 4: Build up, don't tear down

No — I'm not talking about home renovations.

I believe we live in a world where it has become fashionable to tear things apart and be destructive. It seems social media interactions are based on tearing people down and projecting negativity into the world.

As you've seen, I spent more than 30 years of my life slowly burning bridges.

Those bridges are hard to rebuild. So, whenever you get the chance, avoid tearing things down and look solely at building them up.

When you put your head on the pillow each night, ask yourself this question: 'How did I help to build myself, and others, up to be the best they can be?'

Encourage and support your friends and family to take risks. Listen when they speak. Share knowledge with them. Highlight and celebrate their positive traits and qualities. And practise tolerance and acceptance when relationships get tricky.

Lesson 5: It's okay to say you don't know

No-one knows everything — nor do we, or should we, expect this of ourselves. Yet, in personal and professional settings, we're often scared to admit we don't know something.

It's as though not knowing the correct or expected answer is seen as a sign of weakness. Well, it's not. And we need to get rid of that mentality. It's an opportunity for all of us to seek clarity from others or to seek knowledge when we don't know things. This will lead to greater understanding. And to a day when we're less 'wrong', and we 'don't know' ... less.

Lesson 6: Don't buy green bananas

I always say, 'Don't buy green bananas' because you may not be around to see them ripen. Long-term plans are great — and exciting. But try to break the habit of pinning too much hope (too heavily) on your future. In 2019, could any of us have predicted what a year 2020 would become?

I remember teaching alongside a man who put all his eggs and plans in his 'retirement' basket. His goal was to travel the world once he wrapped up teaching. He lived alone, rarely went out and never treated himself to things that excited or fulfilled him at the time.

He was so focused on the life he was going to have that he failed to live the life that he had.

Unfortunately, he died of a heart attack two days after he retired. So, I guess the moral of the story is … live for now.

Don't look for positives you can take out of tomorrow when you can have them today.

Eat well, take baths, sleep in, drink from the container, binge on shows you enjoy and spend 'leisure money' while you have leisurely time to spend it.

To put it bluntly, we'll all be dead a long time. So we might as well live while we can.

Lesson 7: Every choice has a consequence

Always remember that learning provides knowledge, knowledge provides a deeper understanding and understanding provides you with choice. In life you'll always have a choice. But also remember these choices will always have consequences.

» Don't like your job? Fine! Quit — but you may not have money coming in while you look for a better suited position.

» Want to tell someone to go f*#@ themselves? Sure — but what about the relationship you could have potentially formed?

» Did you cut corners on things that were special or meaningful to either your workplace or other people? Your reputation and relationships could be at risk.

I'm not saying don't make choices. But be grateful you have knowledge and understanding. And recognise that every choice you make will have a consequence. Knowing this — and accepting this — will make you better at making decisions. Or preparing for the consequences that come alongside those decisions.

Lesson 8: Be curious, not judgemental

Too often we lack the time, empathy or willingness to truly understand those around us. We develop our assumptions based on the way a person interacts with us or appears to us on singular occasions. And we use those interactions to form judgements instead of being open-minded and curious.

Just like an iceberg, so much substance is hidden in us below the surface. This means we often fail to notice, understand and appreciate what has been instrumental in shaping how a person interacts with the world and others.

So don't base your assumptions on what people show you. Be curious. Ask the why and how questions. Put on your scuba gear and dive. The real treasure lies below.

Lesson 9: Be you

There is nobody like you. You are an exceptional and unique human who has the power to bring happiness to the world and to those around you. You were born loving, and have learned to be honest, respectful and curious. The 'you' that is the best version of *yourself* will always be enough for people. Don't change it. Be fiercely proud of who you are. But if there are things that need changing (for you), then have the courage to change them.

Lesson 10: Treasure what you have

You don't truly appreciate something until it is taken away from you. Living through the COVID-19 pandemic has shown us how quickly our circumstances can change. Many had been accustomed to skipping through life with the sole goal of fulfilling materialist desires — a classier or faster vehicle, a more salubrious abode, the next iPhone or Apple Watch — instead of focusing on what they had and the opportunities present in what was already within arm's reach. Then, COVID-19 well and truly spanked our collective butts! And as we lost freedoms, travel, jobs, homes and health, we realised how lucky we had once been.

It's a true reminder to hold things that matter close.

ONE FINAL CHALLENGE

THIS BOOK HAS BEEN full of stories of incredible highs and occasions of incredible lows. It is an open reflection on my life, my learnings and the way I see adults benefitting from play, which has helped me so dramatically.

So, as you put this book down, I want you to start doing things that either excite, delight or scare you. Get out of your comfort zone. Unlock that inner child and play.

Think about how you can involve family, friends or your workplace. And then tell me your story about how play has brightened your day and the days of those around you.

With a name like Dale Sidebottom, I'm easily reachable (and discoverable) on social media. You don't have to tell me a story of success. It can be a story of learning.

You've heard mine. Now it's time we heard yours.

Dale Sidebottom:

Email: dale@energetic.education
Instagram: @dalesidebottom
Twitter: @dalesidebottom

ACKNOWLEDGEMENTS

IT'S TRUE THAT CREATING a book is never possible without many working sections and many hard-working people. It's a project that fosters connection and opens up new connections along the way.

A book like this (with all my mumbling thoughts) couldn't have been possible without many people. So, I want to take time to thank each individually and purposely because it has taken a lot of commitment, patience and kindness to make it happen.

First of all, I want to extend my gratitude to Richard Cheetham MBE, Professor Alison James and Dr Craig Daly. They contributed immensely to this book, providing research and analysis for themes I have only ever had first-hand experiences with.

Richard Cheetham has a reputation at national and international level in coach education and development in sports ranging from rugby union to slalom canoe and professional cycling with the UCI. Alongside this work has been his continued promotion of and research into the value of play. This has been by encouraging teachers and coaches to recognise its importance in education and sport settings and ensuring it is a key element in the learning environment. Richard received UK Coaching Coach Developer of the year award in 2018.

Sometimes, the powers of social media marvel me. I was connected to Richard via Twitter one day, and we hit it off from there.

Richard was a guest on my podcast and it felt like I was talking to myself — although a much more mature version! Richard is passionate, full of energy and holds play as such an utterly important part of life. He also has an MBE, which is why I was surprised by his patience, openness and willingness to work with me.

Alongside our podcast, Richard and I have now designed special creative play and movement daily mission cards as part of the toolkit of Jugar Life. These cards are something I'm extremely proud of, and I thank you Richard for your friendship, mentorship and comradery, not to mention your contribution to this book.

Alison James is a UK National Teaching Fellow, Principal Fellow of the Higher Education Academy (now Advance HE), an accredited LEGO® Serious Play® facilitator and a professional coach. She is an independent academic writer, adviser and researcher on play and creativity in adult learning. Since 2019 she has been conducting research internationally into the value of play in higher education, funded by the Imagination Lab Foundation, a not-for-profit organisation dedicated to exploring the intersections between the arts, science, management, education, play and imagination. For more information on Alison, please visit engagingimagination.com.

Alison and I are two like-minded individuals. Much like Richard, thanks to the power of the internet and through people's willingness to connect, I have been able to work closely with Richard or Alison without ever having met them in the flesh — although I look forward to a day when I finally can. Alison is a published author and professor. She's incredibly talented, and as your average Joe from the Aussie bush, I feel extremely lucky to have worked with her. Thank you, Alison, for your time, patience and friendship. Alison, your energy and passion for play is something I admire dearly. Thank you from the bottom of my heart.

Craig Daly has been learning about education for more than 30 years, and has spent time in Australia, Japan, Peru, China and South Korea trying to unlock its secret. Originally trained in Queensland, Australia as a teacher with specialisations in both physical education and maths, he experienced education as a classroom and specialist teacher, head of department, learning innovation team lead and school administrator before moving into higher education as a lead academic and consultant in pre-service teacher education. It was during Craig's time as the Head of the Physical Activity, Wellness & Sport (PAWS) group at QUT in Brisbane that his passion for delivering enhanced wellness initiatives was honed. He has extensive educational consultancy experience, having delivered positive outcomes when working with ministerial officials in Malaysia and Nauru, and various administrative teams and teachers at international schools in Asia, Africa and Europe. Craig currently resides in Shekou, China with his wife Kris, a lead teacher, and their rescue dog Lucy. Now mostly retired, he spends the majority of his time completing house husband duties in an astonishingly oversized apartment, and occasionally locks himself into his study to finish writing a book that was due for completion in the summer of 2019.

As you learned during this book, Craig and I met one day in South Korea over a round of screen golf. And as the story suggested, we have been magical mates ever since. Craig: I'm still convinced we're friends because I'm the only witness of your 183.6-metre iron into the 18th hole in Korea. You've cemented my belief in life that you meet people for the right reasons. We get each other. And I've enjoyed every project we have since worked on. Travelling can be lonely but it makes your life richer when you meet mates, such as I have in Craig.

Craig, thank you for your continued support and contribution to this book.

To my beautiful wife **Bree** and our dog **Bluebell**. You both accepted me as part of your already established gang early on. And this was at a time when I was still trying to unlearn the damaging behaviours that led me to a downfall in life.

Bluebell, I once used to get frustrated that more attention would be on you than me. But you have taught me to be patient, empathetic and okay with not always having the spotlight. I know you're a dog — so I'll tell you this via a pat later.

Bree: I have loved falling in love with you. And you have fallen in love with me, even though I make you play silly games time and time again. And often slip up and act selfishly. You've taught me how to put the needs of others before my own. You've given me a family in you and Bluey. You've helped me to slow down and appreciate all those small moments we spend together. Thank you for being you. I love you and am so excited about the family we are creating together.

Thanks for swiping right Breeza.

During the process of writing this book, my life really did change forever. On 10 December 2020 at 11.24 am Bree gave birth to the most beautiful thing I have ever seen — a little baby boy in **Sonny Mack Sidebottom**. People have been telling me for ages that fatherhood is the best thing that will ever happen to you, and I must admit I totally agree. Sonny, I hope this book helps explain the person I was and the person who is now your father. I love you, little man.

To my parents and my two younger sisters: **Kaz**, **Kev**, **Kayla** and **Hannah**. I know we have had our fair share of ups and downs. But I am truly grateful for the patience and kindness you have shown me. Particularly when I wasn't the nicest, most deserving of brothers or son. You all mean the world to me, and I really mean that — even if our board games still end in some tears from time to time.

Through this book, I hope you see the growth and development I have taken not only for myself, but for you all. You have all helped shape (and reshape) the person I am today, and I'll forever be in your favour.

Jarrod Robinson: Two doors down from where I moved to in Ballarat as I was undertaking my teaching degree, I met Jarrod, who has since become the biggest influence and mentor on my career. Jarrod: my successes and achievements have been thoroughly supported by you. You have championed me, and my own business endeavours right from when we were much younger, until now. For that, I'm extremely thankful to you.

And thank you for connecting me with **Carl Condliffe** who has also become a fantastic friend over the years. Carl, even though you're from New Zealand I won't hold it against you!

Jarrod and Carl, I am so grateful for our friendship and the support you both constantly show and give me on a daily basis.

Tarah Miller: I owe a huge thank you to you as you have been on this journey with me from the beginning and for supporting this book from pitch to publication. Not only has Tarah aided in this book coming to life, she has also become a friend over this journey. Tarah is a Communication (PR) Specialist who I met back in 2018 when I wanted support shaping my story, business brand and the overarching idea/theme for this book. (Yes, it has been a dream years in the making!) Reaching out for professional help and advice was a big step for me — and with Tarah's and her director, Jules' help at the time, my vision for the way I had been looking at my business changed. If you haven't had a mentor, coach or even a soundboard to look at things you're working on objectively and with fresh eyes, I strongly recommend that you do this.

Since meeting Tarah, she has become one of my biggest influencers and sounding boards. We're from different industries, but have formed common passion and understanding. **Tarah:** your positivity, your energy and your enthusiasm is something that I have connected with. You're the reason this book looks so good and (hopefully) sounds good. Tarah helped me manage this dream for two-and-a-half years.

Tarah, from the bottom of my heart ... thank you. Thank you so much for believing in me and helping me along the way.

Sandra Balonyi: Thank you for weaving your editorial magic into my words. Your passion and dedication to my vision has been seriously next level. I have loved the process that, to be honest, initially scared the sh*t out of me. But doing it with your guidance, patience and understanding made it an enjoyable journey.

Lucy Raymond and the sensational team at Wiley: Writing a book has been a bloody scary adventure. It hasn't come naturally to me, but you have been with me this entire process, guiding me through it, and I thank you for that.

Since our first meeting it felt like the perfect match. Lucy, you believed in our book idea from the start. You showed faith in me and play-based mindfulness as a concept, and for that I'm so grateful.

To anyone reading this book: If you have got this far, what a great effort! Pat yourselves on the back. May you take something out of it, and pass it on.

And most of all, do everything in your will to conduct your every day with play-based mindfulness, cheerfulness and gratitude. Love the person you see in the mirror and the world will love you back.

Thanks for reading.

INDEX